CHOOSING OPTIONS AND ACCOMMODATIONS FOR CHILDREN

CHOOSING OPTIONS AND ACCOMMODATIONS FOR CHILDREN

COACH

A Guide to Planning Inclusive Education

by

MICHAEL F. GIANGRECO, Ph.D.
Research Assistant Professor
Center for Developmental Disabilities
University of Vermont
Burlington

CHIGEE J. CLONINGER, Ph.D.
Research Associate Professor
Center for Developmental Disabilities
University of Vermont
Burlington

and

VIRGINIA SALCE IVERSON, M.Ed.
Educational Consultant
State of Vermont I-Team
Northwest Region
Essex Junction

·P·A·U·L·H·
BROOKES
PUBLISHING C°

Baltimore • London • Toronto • Sydney

Paul H. Brookes Publishing Co.
P.O. Box 10624
Baltimore, Maryland 21285-0624

All royalties from the sale of this book will be donated to nonprofit agencies who address human needs.

Typeset by Brushwood Graphics, Inc., Baltimore, Maryland.
Manufactured in the United States of America by
BookCrafters, Falls Church, Virginia.

Second printing, September 1993.
Third printing, September 1994.

Library of Congress Cataloging-in-Publication Data
Giangreco, Michael F., 1956–
    Choosing options and accommodations for children
    (COACH) : a guide to planning inclusive education / by Michael F.
    Giangreco, Chigee J. Cloninger, Virginia Salce Iverson.
        p.   cm.
Includes bibliographical references (p.   ) and index.
ISBN 1-55766-106-5
1. Mainstreaming in education—United States.   2. Handicapped
children—Education—United States.   3. Home and school—
United States.   4. Quality of life—United States.   I. Cloninger,
Chigee J., 1946–   . II. Iverson, Virginia Salce, 1951–   . III. Title.
LC4031.G5   1992   92-28405
371.9'046'0973–dc20   CIP

(British Library Cataloguing-in-Publication data are available
from the British Library.)

CONTENTS

FOREWORD

Change is constant. It involves a process of learning and growing. It involves struggle and is resisted by many. Change is necessary to move forward in our understanding and practice in working toward students becoming fully included in school and community life. More broadly, change is necessary if we are to understand more fully how communities of people can live and learn together. Perhaps one of the most hopeful opportunities afforded through the use of processes such as Choosing Options and Accommodations for Children (COACH) is that people learn to work together toward a common goal: belonging and learning in inclusive school communities.

Exemplary practices for educational services for students with disabilities have changed dramatically in the 17 years since the passing of Public Law 94-142, the Education for All Handicapped Children Act of 1975. The changes are characterized by shifts in:

- *Location*—from segregated settings to integrated or inclusive settings
- *Curriculum*—from developmental and remedial designs to ecological and functional designs
- *Instruction*—from isolated and highly controlled contexts to natural contexts with a greater recognition of incidental and problem-solving approaches
- *Teamwork*—from isolated and multidisciplinary models to more integrated and collaborative ways of working together
- *Family involvement*—from the role of approver of priorities pre-determined by professionals to the role of co-designer of educational programs.

Each shift or progression in the conceptualization of educational service design creates the need to develop practices and procedures that operationalize the concepts and philosophies into day-to-day practice.

One of the most dramatic shifts from the mid-1980s into the early 1990s has been the effort physically, socially, and programmatically to include students with disabilities who have significant support needs in general education classes and other aspects of school and community life. This shift out of isolation and into the mainstream has resulted in the need for substantial changes in curricular design, instructional methods, and the roles and functions of general educators, special educators, and related services personnel. Uncertainty of how to proceed is evidenced in the range of questions frequently posed by families and educators alike: "What should Ramon do in 8th grade earth science? How will Keisha's functional needs be met in the academic portions of 3rd grade? Can Adam ever be pulled out of regular instruction to work in a small group? When should we initiate instruction in off-campus community sites? What related services are necessary; where and when will they be provided?" There are no recipes or roadmaps, and certainly there are no generic right or wrong answers. The answers will vary depending on the unique learning and social needs of individual students and depending on the particular school and community contexts. Arriving at the answers requires participation in a thoughtful process and an exchange of information among the individuals who know the students best and who have vested, long-term interests. A consensus decision-making process for the key people in an individual student's life is firmly rooted in COACH.

The COACH process operationalizes the principles of individualization, family–school partnerships, school and community inclusion, and collaborative teamwork. It is an invaluable resource for addressing implementation of an inclusive educational program. Particularly valuable aspects of COACH include:

- A process that both requires and extends essential partnerships between family members and school personnel in program design

- A curricular design focused on attainment of valued life outcomes, not acquisition of fragmented and isolated skills
- A broad conceptualization of curriculum that encompasses all potential learning needs and opportunities in home, school, and community environments
- A process that promotes the provision of special education and related services that support educational programs in inclusive contexts after educational priorities are established for students
- Active involvement of a variety of disciplines through a process that maintains a whole-child and ecological perspective, as opposed to maintaining discipline-specific perspectives and priorities
- The use of alternating divergent and convergent thought processes that result in a valid and reliable set of individualized education priorities
- Attention to both learner outcome and essential support aspects of program design and implementation

COACH is a tool for moving beyond the philosophy of inclusion to engaging in a process that is practical, yet comprehensive, for designing and implementing individualized education programs (IEPs) for students with disabilities in inclusive school communities. COACH creates mechanisms for teams to establish a shared framework, develop unified goals, and make consensus decisions about the content of the student's educational program.

The COACH process may seem overwhelming at first because it is very detailed and explicit. These characteristics are two of its greatest assets. Just as Giangreco and his colleagues caution teams to identify reasonable expectations for individual student programs given the amount of available instruction time, during initial use of the COACH process your team is encouraged to determine manageable ways to learn the process. For example, work through the entire process with one or two students before using it on a wider scale. Through this experiential learning, you will become more efficient working together as a team in the application of the process. Keep in mind that the COACH process represents over 7 years of field testing in collaboration with families and educators in numerous communities. Newcomers to the process should not despair if unable to grasp every detail but rejoice that a comprehensive process exists for use as a guide to curriculum development.

With our collective belief that a major function of schools is to teach children about themselves, others, and the world around them, we must continue to learn and grow in our knowledge about how to accomplish this critically important task. Moving forward requires taking risks, which, unfortunately, occurs far too little in our greatly bureaucratized schools. Often, it is helpful to have a process that others have found useful as a framework to structure new learning. COACH is such a process and is sure to support many teams as they work to figure out how to create their own inclusive school communities that maximize learning for all children. Dissemination of COACH is particularly timely now given increasing knowledge that collaboration will be the cornerstone of quality educational services and supports for years to come.

Jennifer York, Ph.D., P.T.
Assistant Professor of Educational Psychology
Coordinator for Interdisciplinary Preservice Programs
Institute on Community Integration
University of Minnesota

and

Terri Vandercook, Ph.D.
Director of Inclusive Education Programs
Institute on Community Integration
University of Minnesota

PREFACE

COACH originated in 1982 as an unnamed tool to assist in planning individualized habilitation plans for adults with disabilities who were living in the community. At the time, it reflected a combination of the field's most promising practices. But much of what was considered exemplary in 1982 is outdated now. In 1985, the tool was revised for use in public school programs serving students with disabilities and was given the name COACH. From 1985 to 1990, COACH stood for Cayuga-Onondaga Assessment for Children with Handicaps. It was named after the place where it continued to be developed, Cayuga and Onondaga counties in central New York State. From 1985 until the present, COACH was updated annually to reflect current exemplary practices in the field, as well as feedback from parents, students, teachers, related services professionals, and administrators from across the United States and Canada. Since joining the faculty at the University of Vermont in 1988, my colleagues Chigee Cloninger and Virginia Iverson have assisted me in updating the last three versions of COACH. Field testing since 1988 has occurred extensively in settings where students with disabilities are educated in general education classes in their neighborhood schools.

Those who have used previous versions of COACH will notice that the meaning of the acronym has changed to Choosing Options and Accommodations for Children. This title change is more descriptive of the purpose of COACH and eliminates the word "handicaps," which has been completely omitted from the Individuals with Disabilities Education Act of 1990 (Public Law 101-476).

Part 1 of COACH (the Family Prioritization Interview) has been reorganized. Its content is more explicitly referenced to valued life outcomes for students. Changes in Part 1 make it more family-centered as well as easier and faster to use. Part 2 (Directions for Defining the Educational Program Components) has been explained more thoroughly, as has Part 3 (Addressing the Educational Program Components in Inclusive Settings). A scoring key and list of valued life outcomes for use during the Family Prioritization Interview are available in Appendix A. Blank forms for COACH are available in Appendix B. The Self-Monitoring and Peer Coaching Guide to COACH has been added in Appendix C to assist in increasing your proficiency with COACH. Examples of completed forms are provided to illustrate the use of COACH with students of different ages and challenges (Appendices D and E). **The reader has permission to photocopy any material from Appendices A, B, and C in this book.**

As with any tool, the successful use of COACH is dependent upon the skill of its user. To use COACH effectively, you must:

1. Read the manual completely before attempting to use any part of COACH.
2. Become familiar with the assumptions upon which COACH is based. Understanding the philosophical underpinnings of COACH will help you decide whether to use it. Familiarity with the assumptions, especially those pertaining to the processes embedded in COACH, will help you tailor its use to individual families.
3. Develop a team plan that explains how COACH fits into the team's overall efforts on behalf of a student.
4. Understand that Parts 1 and 2 are conceptually and practically linked. Completing Part 1 without completing Part 2 is like building a car that has an engine but no body. The engine may be of superior quality, but the car simply will not do what you want it to without the other parts that make it a whole car. Parts 1 and 2 of COACH create a picture of what a whole educational program for a student looks like. Parts 1 and 2 deal exclusively with the "what" of the educational program, not the "how." Although Part 3 is logically linked to Parts 1 and 2, it has a level of independence. Much of Part 3 is useful only in situations in which students receive special edu-

cation services in general education classrooms or are being transitioned into general education classrooms. You can generate the information needed to complete Part 3 successfully by using COACH Parts 1 and 2 or by using other tools that generate the same type of information.

5. Work collaboratively with your teammates to increase your proficiency with COACH using the Self-Monitoring and Peer Coaching Guide to COACH (Appendix C).

Good Luck!

Michael F. Giangreco, Ph.D.

ACKNOWLEDGMENTS

The number of people who deserve special thanks for contributing to the development and field testing of COACH from 1982 to 1992 are too numerous to mention by name. Many of the most significant contributors have been affiliated with the Center for Developmental Disabilities at the University of Vermont in Burlington; members of the Vermont State Interdisciplinary Team for Intensive Special Education; colleagues, school staff, and families throughout the United States and Canada; and staff of the Cayuga-Onondaga Board of Cooperative Educational Services (BOCES) in Auburn, New York. Thanks to all of the people who offered their ideas and support. We wish to extend a special thank you to Natalie Tyler of Paul H. Brookes Publishing Company for her many hours of work making this book a reality.

With love and thanks
to members of our families—

Guy and Maryann Giangreco
Dan and Melanie Giangreco

Pete Murphy
Marjorie and Dobbin (R.D.) Cloninger

Craig, Colin, and Courtney Iverson
Dora Salce
Linda Salce McCarthy

CHOOSING OPTIONS AND ACCOMMODATIONS FOR CHILDREN

COACH

SECTION I

INTRODUCTION

INTRODUCTION

Across North America and around the world, families and professionals are discussing the merits of educating students with disabilities with their peers who do not have disabilities in general education classrooms. This movement toward full inclusion is accompanied by a wealth of information explaining the rationale and benefits of inclusive education for students with varied challenges and needs (Forest, 1984, 1987; Fox & Williams, 1991a; Gartner & Lipsky, 1987, 1989; Giangreco & Meyer, 1988; Giangreco & Putnam, 1991; Lipsky & Gartner, 1989; Meyer, Peck, & Brown, 1991; Peck, Donaldson, & Pezzoli; Salisbury, 1991; Schaffner & Buswell, 1991; Stainback & Stainback, 1990, 1992; Stainback, Stainback, & Forest, 1989; Strully & Strully, 1985; Taylor, 1988; York & Vandercook, 1990).

Only since the 1980s have practical tools emerged that are specifically designed to operationalize various aspects of full inclusion and exemplary educational practices. Many people who support inclusive education still want to know **how to accomplish it**. Inclusion requires more than merely being physically present in a general education classroom. Quality inclusion requires the development and implementation of educational plans that meet individual students' needs in inclusive environments. Whether students' needs have been met is reflected not only by whether they have attained certain objectives, but by the impact that educational experiences have had on their lives. By referencing the student's educational program to the characteristics of a good quality of life, we remain mindful of our shared desire that the lives of children we teach be bettered as a result of their having been in school.

Although criterion-referenced and norm-referenced assessment tools may have some value in determining a student's level of functioning, these tools rarely offer guidelines for using this information to assist with planning educational programs that enhance valued life outcomes. Often, these same tools lead consumers through detailed assessment of a huge number of items that may, or may not, be part of the student's educational program in the near future. Some comprehensive assessment tools take days to complete for each student, yet the results are not directly useful for planning the student's educational program. Frequently, this occurs because these assessment tools are not designed for planning purposes or the tools do not include steps that explicitly link the assessment results to planning the educational program.

Choosing Options and Accommodations for Children (COACH) offers an alternative to traditional criterion-referenced assessment approaches. COACH is an **assessment and planning tool** designed to identify the content of a student's educational program for implementation in general education settings and activities based on individually determined valued life outcomes. COACH is organized into three major parts. **Part 1 (Family Prioritization Interview)** is used to identify family-centered priorities for the student. **Part 2 (Defining the Educational Program Components)** is used to develop annual goals and short-term objectives based on family-centered priorities, identify other learning outcomes beyond the family-centered priorities, and determine general supports and accommodations needed for a student to participate in his educational program. **Part 3 (Addressing the Educational Program Components in Inclusive Settings)** is used to determine options for addressing students' educational program components in general education class settings through the use of a scheduling matrix and a set of instructional guidelines. These three major parts of COACH are interdependent.

In recognition of the importance of using language that is respectful of people with disabilities, this book contains person-first language, so that reference to a person (e.g., child, student, teenager) always precedes any disability descriptor (e.g., developmental disabilities, autism). Additionally, to avoid awkward constructions such as *his or her* and *he or she*, we have chosen to alternate female and male pronouns throughout the text.

ASSUMPTIONS FORMING THE BASIS OF COACH

This section describes six assumptions upon which COACH is based: 1) pursuing valued life outcomes is an important aspect of education; 2) the family is the cornerstone of relevant and longitudinal educational planning; 3) collaborative teamwork is essential to quality education; 4) coordinated planning is dependent upon shared, discipline-free goals; 5) using problem-solving methods improves the effectiveness of educational planning; and 6) special education is a service, not a place.

1.   Pursuing Valued Life Outcomes Is an Important Aspect of Education

Since the 1980s there has been an increased emphasis on ensuring good quality of life for people with disabilities (Bradley & Knoll, in press; Fabian, 1991; Horner, 1991). The professional literature (Bogdan & Taylor, 1987; Kennedy, Killius, & Olson, 1987; Meyer et al., 1991; Schalock, 1990), field testing done for earlier versions of COACH, and interviews with parents whose children have disabilities (Giangreco, Cloninger, Mueller, Yuan, & Ashworth, 1991) have highlighted five major valued life outcomes that exemplify a good quality of life. COACH provides a means to connect valued life outcomes to the design and implementation of a student's educational program. These valued life outcomes are:

1.   Having a safe, stable home in which to live now and/or in the future
2.   Having access to a variety of places and engaging in meaningful activities
3.   Having a social network of personally meaningful relationships
4.   Having a level of personal choice and control that matches one's age
5.   Being safe and healthy

For an individual student, these valued life outcomes are meant to provide a balance between independence and interdependence with others. Each of these valued life outcomes will hold different meanings to different individual families. Few people would dispute that pursuing valued life outcomes is an important goal of our educational system. However, the professional literature offers few approaches to or examples of educational assessment and planning that actively connect a student's educational programs to these or other valued life outcomes.

While there may be general agreement about what constitutes basic valued life outcomes, how best to assess, plan for, and pursue these relevant outcomes through education remains debatable. One approach follows the logic that increasing independence in performing daily living skills will lead to valued life outcomes. While this may be true, there is no guarantee that skill development necessarily leads to improvement in a person's valued life outcomes. For instance, teaching banking skills to a student who will have little opportunity or need to use them may have no impact on that individual. For another student (e.g., a teenager with a job), learning to use an automated teller machine may mean more choice, control, or independence. Another approach is that a student's valued life outcomes can be improved when people provide supports for the individual. This approach requires changes in the student's physical or social environment and little or no change in student behavior. For example, teaching a student's classmates how to communicate with her using an augmentative communication method may result in increased social interactions and friendships without the student having to gain additional communication skills.

COACH is based on the assumption that some combination of skill development by the student and supports provided by others is needed to improve valued life outcomes for most students. The balance between these two aspects of education—skill development and supports—is determined based on their relationship to the needs of individual students and their families. Developing educational programs that are linked directly to students' valued life outcomes is a shift from traditional approaches, which assume that skill development alone is sufficient to pursue a better life (Bradley & Knoll, in press).

COACH provides a method for exploring a student's current valued life outcomes and the family's hopes for future directions. The student herself, as part of the family, is included in this process whenever this is appropriate. Every effort should be made to consider the wishes of individuals to make their own decisions, regardless of their level of perceived ability. We suggest that the amount of involvement for each student be considered individually and follow typical patterns for children without disabilities. Generally, this means that when students are young, parents have greater control; as the child grows older, the control is gradually shifted. Thus, as the student becomes a young adult she has ongoing opportunities to prepare herself to make her own choices about increasingly important and personal issues (e.g., living arrangements, employment, relationships).

As consumers, families are relied upon to offer the vision for the child's current and future valued life outcomes, based on their personal values and desires. Having the family establish this individualized vision of what they value sets a meaningful context for educational planning by allowing for the development of educational programs designed to support the family.

The following section describes and explains the five valued life outcomes. It is important to realize that different families will attach a different meaning to each outcome. These descriptions offer examples of how some families have interpreted the outcome; this does not infer that a family using COACH must match any of the examples. It is also crucial to remember that valued life outcomes may be pursued by the student developing skills and by those who interact with the student providing supports.

Having a Safe, Stable Home in Which To Live Now and/or in the Future "Home" means a place of belonging, security, safety, privacy, and where you can feel free to be yourself. Luckily, many children in North America grow up in safe, stable homes with at least one parent or family member. For them, remaining in a safe, stable home during their school years is not an issue. These families care for their children unconditionally and expect to provide a home for them at least until adulthood. However, this is not true for all children. Some children, through no fault of their own, do not have families or homes in which to live. They may reside in institutions, large group homes, nursing homes, or may move from one foster family to another. An increasing number of children in North America are homeless along with their parents, brothers, and sisters. Obviously, such situations hurt children and families. Other children may live at home but present serious challenges to their family's capacity to provide for their unique physical, behavioral, or medical needs. At times, the needs of the child and the needs of the family may be in conflict.

For some children, the outcome of having a home refers to enabling a person to **continue** living in a safe, stable, home. For example, a teenager with severe behavioral challenges may be at risk for placement outside his home because he is aggressive toward family members. Having this young man learn new skills to control his own behavior, or providing supports to the parents (e.g., respite care, counseling) may have an impact on the family's ability to raise him at home. Another teenager who has severe physical challenges may be easier to maintain at home if she learns certain skills (e.g., how to assist in self-care activities) or if needed supports (e.g., specialized equipment) are made available.

For other children, the outcome of having a home refers to allowing a person access to a safe, stable home either now or in the future. This is most commonly a concern as the family ages and the child becomes a young adult. For example, Jai may have had a wonderful home growing up with his parents, sisters, and brothers. But both Jai and his parents hope that when Jai is a young adult he will be able to live in an apartment with a friend as a roommate. Jai and his family may be able to increase the probability of realizing that goal if Jai learns certain skills, such as responding to a smoke alarm, preparing his own food, and being able to make purchases. Since valued life outcomes can also be strengthened through supports we provide to people, Jai's access to the opportunity to live in his own apartment need not be predicated on skill development. Supports can be provided to Jai (e.g., attendant care) so that living in an apartment with a roommate becomes a reality regardless of his skill development.

Having Access to a Variety of Places and Engaging in Meaningful Activities Going to a variety of places, regardless of the level of one's participation, is part of what separates a boring existence from an interesting life. In this context, "places" refers to any variety of locations used by people without disabilities, such as friends' homes, stores, parks, restaurants, and work sites. "Meaningful activities" refers to activities that are valued by both society and the individual. "Valued by the individual" means that the activity is a preference or interest of the person or makes the person feel good about herself. These activities may be intrinsically valued by the person as in the fun of swimming, or may have some secondary value to the person, as in earning money for doing chores. For different people, work fits in one or both of these categories. Some people like their work and feel good about themselves because they work. For others, the work itself is not highly valued, but the pay it brings is. Parents tell us that their childrens' lives are improved as participation in meaningful activities at inclusive places is expanded (Giangreco, Cloninger, et al., 1991).

Having a Social Network of Personally Meaningful Relationships Although most people appreciate some time alone, people also can suffer the effects of isolation and loneliness if they do not have a network of meaningful relationships. Additionally, the absence of a social network can put enormous stress on the small existing network which often is the nuclear family. Most people highly value their relationships and interactions with other people, and, in part, define themselves by the people with whom they affiliate. Having personally meaningful relationships is a valued component of most people's lives.

Having a Level of Personal Choice and Control that Matches One's Age Some people with disabilities have less personal choice and control than people without disabilities of the same age. For example, it is not unusual to observe a youngster with severe physical or cognitive disabilities who has little or no control over important, or even mundane, aspects of his daily life. Someone else may decide when he gets out of bed, what he eats, what he wears, where he goes, how long he stays, whom he will see, when he will get out of his wheelchair, what he will play with, where he will live and with whom, where he will work, or whether he will work at all. There is a concern that such lack of choice may lead to learned helplessness, so that the person becomes resigned to his plight, lacking the will to challenge others' control over aspects of life that many people without disabilities take for granted. For others, lack of choice may lead to actively challenging behaviors (e.g., aggression). While we do not presume to know the thoughts behind the actions or inactions of people with severe disabilities, allowing people a chronological age–appropriate level of choice and control is consistent with Donnellan's (1984) **criterion of the least dangerous assumption**. If we are not sure about the motivations or intentions of an individual, we are safer to err on the side of providing opportunities for choice and control.

Being Safe and Healthy Personal safety and health are foundational outcomes. Similar to other valued life outcomes, safety and health can be enhanced by the supports we provide for people as well as skill development on the part of the person. Frequently, safety and health issues overlap other valued life outcomes. For example, learning pedestrian skills may address **access** to new places and **safety** to minimize the chance of being hit by a car, as well as expanded **choices**. Learning to respond to an emergency alarm may improve safety as well as improving access to certain types of living arrangements. We can affect peoples' personal health and wellness through the foods they eat, the care we take to ensure that their specialized equipment is properly fitted, or the exercise and fitness activities we teach them. Safety and health frequently must be balanced with choice, control, and independence. With new choices come new physical and emotional risks to safety, ranging from the pain of a broken bone to the pain of a broken heart. The balance between safety/ health and personal choice should be determined by each family and include the student.

2.   The Family Is the Cornerstone of Relevant and Longitudinal Educational Planning

One aim of COACH is to assist families in becoming better consumers of education and related services, as well as partners in the educational process. This emphasis on consumerism and partnership is based on the following five beliefs:

Families Know Certain Aspects of Their Children Better than Anyone Else Although teachers and other school staff observe students throughout a 5- to 6-hour school day, this is only a fraction of a student's entire day. The rest of that day, as well as weekends, holidays, and summer vacations, present a more complete picture of the student's life. As educators, we must remind ourselves that we spend only about half the days of the year with our students, seeing them less than a third of each of those days. Parents, brothers, sisters, and others are present for much of the student's nonschool time. Nonschool time may provide key information that has educational implications, such as the nature of the student's interests, motivations, habits, fears, routines, pressures, needs, and health. By listening to parents, educators can gain a more complete understanding of the student's life outside school.

Families Have the Greatest Vested Interest in Seeing Their Children Learn In our professional eagerness to help children learn, we sometimes convey a message to parents that teachers care more about their children than they do. Of course, this is rarely the case. It can be dangerous to make assumptions about a parent's intentions based on certain behaviors. One study of parents of children with multiple disabilities sheds light on why some mothers and fathers withdraw from the educational process (e.g., choose not to attend educational meetings). As one parent said, "It doesn't matter what I say because they [professionals] are going to do what they want anyway" (Giangreco, Cloninger, et al., 1991, p. 20). COACH attempts to address this problem by providing a forum and a process that enables families to share their ideas and encourages professionals to listen.

The Family Is Likely To Be the Only Group of Adults Involved with a Child's Educational Program Throughout His or Her Entire School Career Over the course of a school career, a student with special educational needs will encounter so many professionals that it will be difficult for the family to remember all their names. Some of these professionals will work with the child for years, others for a year or less. Eventually, even the most caring of them will depart because they are professionals who are paid to be part of the student's life (Forest & Lusthaus, 1989). However, all of these professionals will bring with them unique skills and ideas that can have a positive effect on the child and family. While such diversity can be healthy if it is well coordinated, the varying input of professionals could prove to be harmful if it is so random and chaotic that it offers no real form or direction. Professionals must build upon a family-centered vision for the child, rather than re-invent a student's educational program each year. Throughout a student's school career, the family is most likely to be the only human constant. Powell and Gallagher (1993) remind us that, typically, brothers and sisters are the people with whom we have our longest relationships, which are longer than even those with parents or friends. Therefore, when we think about the family, we need to consider the child, the parents, siblings, and others who make up her inner circles (Forest & Lusthaus, 1989). COACH is designed to assist families in clarifying and articulating their own changing visions for themselves and their children.

Families Have the Ability To Influence Positively the Quality of Educational Services Provided in Their Community Historically, families have been responsible for improving access to educational and community-based opportunities for their children with disabilities. In the 1950s and 1960s, when schooling was unavailable to many children with disabilities, parents created schools themselves. Families were a driving force behind the passage of the Education for All Handicapped Children Act of 1975, PL 94-142, which mandated a free, appropriate education for all children. Families were influential in the reauthorization of PL 94-142 as the Individuals with Disabilities Education Act of 1990, PL 101-476. Active parent groups and individual families are leading the movement toward full inclusion in general education schools and classrooms. Undoubtedly, families will continue to play a vital role in improving educational services for children with disabilities.

Families Must Live with the Outcomes of Decisions Made by Educational Teams All Day, Every Day People rarely appreciate someone making decisions that will affect their lives, without including them in the decision-making. When families do not do what professionals have prescribed, this may be an indication that the family was inadequately involved in the decision-making process. As professionals, when we make decisions we must constantly remind ourselves that they are likely to affect other people besides the child and to have an effect outside of school. COACH encourages families to be part of the process of deciding what their children's educational program will look like, because they know what the child and family need, what is most important, and what the family can handle. In our experience, when given the opportunity to participate in educational planning using COACH, families can play an invaluable role in determining appropriate educational experiences and can do an excellent job of pinpointing priorities.

3. Collaborative Teamwork Is Essential to Quality Education

COACH is predicated upon family members and professionals working as a team. Teamwork requires some face-to-face interactions, distribution of labor agreed to by the team, and consensus decision-making regarding the explicitly defined components of the educational program.

The goals of educational teams are to design, implement, and evaluate a student's individualized education program (IEP) to pursue valued life outcomes. Specifically, team members have a wide variety of responsibilities such as developing lesson plans, preparing materials, monitoring and evaluating student progress, providing supports, synthesizing the input of educational and related service staff, adapting curriculum, scheduling, communicating with parents, training each other and receiving training, providing peer support, and completing required paperwork (e.g., IEPs, progress reports).

Teams should include those people affected by the decisions made by the team and those who have information or skills to help the team make better decisions (Thousand & Villa, 1992). Teams frequently include parents, the student, general education teachers, special education teachers, related service providers, and paraprofessionals. Since including all these potential members may create a team so large that it has difficulty functioning, some schools have organized themselves into various types of teams. For example, the small group of people who interact with the student daily is sometimes referred to as the **core team**. This group may include the parents, teacher (general and special education), and instructional assistant. An **extended team** includes all core members in addition to those who interact with the student on a less frequent basis, such as itinerant specialists (e.g., occupational therapist, physical therapist, communication specialist). In order to maintain a reasonable group size and use team members' time efficiently, **subteams** formed by any logical combination of team members may be continually created and dissolved to address specific student needs (Skrtic, 1991; Thousand & Villa, 1990).

Some schools have successfully included peers as planning team members or classroom problem-solvers; this is based, in part, on the assumption that classmates have student-centered perspectives that could generate relevant and creative ideas (Giangreco, 1993). Giangreco and Putnam (1991) suggested that the use of peers in educational planning is a promising practice, yet little is currently known about the effects of peer involvement on the planning process or individual students. Since few procedures or guidelines exist describing the involvement of peers in planning, teams are encouraged to design models for peer involvement which pursue intended benefits and establish safeguards for the wishes and dignity of all students involved as team members. Three examples of safeguards are: 1) asking the student with special needs and/or the family if they want peers as part of the planning team, and at what level of involvement; 2) asking for volunteer students who are interested in being team members and then obtaining their parents' permission; and 3) making peers available to support all types of students, not just those with identified disabilities.

Hutchinson (1978) reminded us that "calling a small group of people a team does not make them so" (p. 70). Merely bringing together many people does not ensure that the group will function as a team. Two foundational characteristics of teams are developing a shared framework to pursue a unified set of goals and reaching consensus decisions based on those goals (Giangreco, Edelman, & Dennis, 1991). COACH creates mechanisms for teams to establish a shared framework, develop unified goals, and make consensus decisions about the content of the student's educational program.

One review of the literature (Giangreco, 1989, Chapter 2), indicated that effective teams have certain basic characteristics. Effective teams:

1. Have **two or more members** who possess various skills that may serve different functions, therefore allowing the body of theory and skills to be enlarged.
2. Develop a **shared framework** and purposefully **pursue a unified set of goals**.
3. Engage in **problem-solving** and **collaborative activities** to reach shared goals.
4. **Share and allocate resources** to help the learner attain her goals.
5. Have **participatory interactions** designed to complement each other and improve effectiveness.
6. Serve a collective **evaluation function** and offer each other **feedback**.

7. **Judge success or failure by group performance** toward the unified set of goals, rather than by the individual member's performance.

4. Coordinated Planning Is Dependent upon Shared, Discipline-Free Goals

The selection of **educational learning outcomes and supports for students should be discipline-free**. This means students' learning outcomes and supports should *not* be selected on the basis of what is valued by professionals from various disciplines (e.g., physical therapy [PT], occupational therapy [OT], speech-language pathology, orientation and mobility). Rather, learning outcomes and supports should be selected based on family-centered priorities and valued life outcomes that are individually determined. Agreeing to pursue a shared, discipline-free set of goals for a student is based on the assumption that when professionals pursue separate goals (e.g., PT goals, OT goals, speech goals), the likelihood increases that students' educational experiences will be disjointed, be less relevant, have gaps or overlaps in service, or be contradictory. When families and professionals work together to select and implement a shared set of discipline-free goals, it increases the likelihood that students' education experiences will be more cohesive and relevant, and that services will be delivered in a manner that will assist students in attaining their goals and pursuing valued life outcomes.

Related services personnel often ask where the therapy goals are in COACH. COACH assumes that related services should be provided to enable students to pursue **family-centered, discipline-free IEP goals as the focus of their educational programs, other relevant learning outcomes that provide for a well-rounded school experience, and general supports identified through the use of COACH or other tools**. This assumption is based on the definition of "related services" as described in the Individuals with Disabilities Education Act (IDEA) of 1990 (PL 101-476), which states:

> The term "related services" means transportation and such developmental, corrective, and other supportive services (including speech pathology and audiology, psychological services, physical and occupational therapy, recreation, therapeutic recreation and social work services, and medical and counseling services, including rehabilitation counseling, except that such medical services shall be for diagnostic and evaluation purposes only) **as may be required to assist a child with a disability to benefit from special education** [emphasis added], and includes early identification and assessment of disabling conditions in children. (1401[a][17])

Once these educational program components have been identified, it then becomes appropriate for the team to ask, "In what ways are related services **required** to assist the student in gaining access to identified components of the educational program (i.e., discipline-free goals, other learning outcomes, general supports)?" Knowing the components of the educational program can assist team members in determining: 1) if a related service is needed, 2) what type of service delivery mode (e.g., direct, indirect) is most appropriate, 3) what specialized techniques or methods are appropriate and socially valid, or 4) how the potential delivery of a related service is interdependent with other educational and related services. For more in-depth discussion regarding integrated delivery of related services, refer to Giangreco (1986a, 1986b, 1990a, 1990b, in press); Giangreco, Edelman, and Dennis (1991); Giangreco, York, and Rainforth (1989); Orelove and Sobsey (1991); Rainforth and York (1987); Rainforth, York, and Macdonald (1992); York, Giangreco, Vandercook, and Macdonald (1992); and York, Rainforth, and Giangreco (1990).

5. Using Problem-Solving Methods Improves the Effectiveness of Educational Planning

Developing a relevant educational program for a student with disabilities can be a challenge or, in a sense, a problem to be solved. Professionals with good intentions often seek input from families, but fail to provide them with methods to help them make important decisions. Use of open-ended questions, such as, "What would you like to see on Anthony's IEP this year?" or "What are your priorities for Keisha?" often result in parents deferring to professionals or making selections that do not necessarily represent their top priorities. This may occur because families are faced with trying to prioritize hundreds of options without any strategies to help them organize the vast array of possibilities. While the use of any problem-solving method will not guarantee positive results, it should improve the odds for them.

Unique to COACH is its use of the **Osborn-Parnes Creative Problem Solving (CPS) Process** (Osborn, 1953; Parnes, 1981, 1985, 1988). Aspects of the CPS Process are infused in COACH to help families select the most important learning outcomes to be included on their children's IEPs. Once a person or group has identified a general problem, they can employ the Osborn-Parnes Creative Problem Solving Process, which includes five basic steps: 1) Fact-Finding (gathering information), 2) Problem-Finding (clarifying the problem), 3) Idea-Finding (brainstorming a quantity of ideas in an atmosphere of deferred judgment), 4) Solution-Finding (selecting the best ideas based on criteria), and 5) Acceptance-Finding (making a plan of what to do next and taking action).

An overarching characteristic of the CPS process is the alternating use of divergent and convergent thinking phases. The divergent aspects encourage the problem-solver to explore information and ideas broadly by extending in different directions from a common point. Convergent aspects encourage analysis of the divergent data to make decisions or select solutions. While COACH does not employ a classic application of the CPS process, it retains many of its key features (e.g., certain types of fact-finding, selecting solutions based on criteria). The following section describes how key concepts of the Osborn-Parnes Creative Problem Solving Process are embedded in COACH.

Deferring Judgment   The steps of COACH establish a pattern when participants defer judgment and other times when they actively make judgments. This creates opportunities for parents and other team members to share information in an atmosphere of trust without fear of being criticized or interrupted. Furthermore, it allows for consideration of ideas that might be lost if judged prematurely.

Alternating Between Divergent and Convergent Steps   COACH alternates between divergent and convergent steps. Part 1 (Family Prioritization Interview) begins divergently by setting a context and considering many possibilities. Part 1 ends with the selection of the top priorities for inclusion on the IEP. Once those priorities are determined, Part 2 (Defining the Educational Program Components) reexamines each priority divergently before converging them for restatement as annual goals, and developing short-term objectives. Part 2 also examines other curricular content and student needs divergently before converging them for the selection of additional learning outcomes and general supports. In Part 3 (Addressing the Educational Program Components in Inclusive Settings), divergent possibilities are explored for meeting students' educational needs in inclusive settings. Convergence occurs when a student schedule is written and lesson plans, including specific lesson adaptations, are developed.

Multiple Opportunities and Various Perspectives   COACH helps families select priorities by providing opportunities for parents and team members to consider the large number of possibilities from various perspectives, in smaller and different sets, multiple times, prior to final selection. In traditional approaches, such as asking, "What would you like to see on Miguel's IEP this year?" parents have a single chance to respond. Through COACH, by the time an activity has been selected as a priority for inclusion on the IEP at the end of Part 1 (Family Prioritization Interview), it has been considered by the parent six to nine different times. This increases the likelihood that families will select those activities that truly are priorities for their children. Similarly, Part 2 (Defining the Educational Program Components) and Part 3 (Addressing the Educational Program Components in Inclusive Settings) offer multiple opportunities for team members, including the family, to consider many educational program components before they are selected.

6. Special Education Is a Service, Not a Place

The authors of COACH favor educating students with disabilities in general education classes and other inclusive settings (e.g., community vocational site). This perspective is based in part on our understanding of PL 101-476 (IDEA, 1990), which states, "The term 'special education' means specially designed instruction . . . " (1401[a][16]).

> The law also requires each state to establish procedural safeguards. . . . to assure that, to the maximum extent appropriate, children with disabilities, including children in public or private institutions or other

care facilities, are educated with children who are not disabled, and that special classes, separate schooling, or other removal of children with disabilities from regular education environments occurs only when the nature of severity of the disability is such that education in regular classes with the use of supplementary aids and services cannot be achieved satisfactorily. . . . (1412[5][B])

We interpret this to mean that **special education is a service, not a place**, and that schools must attempt to teach students in inclusive settings with supplemental supports and services before considering more restrictive options (Gartner & Lipsky, 1989; Laski, 1991; Taylor, 1988). In many places, students are removed from general education schools and classrooms, or never allowed initial access to such settings, when they function at a level that is deemed significantly different from the norm for their age. In the authors' experience, students with all types of challenges and needs can be successfully educated in general education environments. Interestingly, the public law does not say that a student should be removed from a general education class if he or she is not doing a level of work similar to that of other students the same age. The obligation of the school is to **provide an appropriate education in what the law terms the least restrictive environment**. Increasingly, there are demonstrations in North America of education in what are now referred to as inclusive environments, showing that students who function at academic and functional levels that are significantly different from those of their peers can receive appropriate educational services in general education classes given appropriate supports (e.g., Berres & Knoblock, 1987; Forest, 1987; Giangreco, Dennis, Cloninger, Edelman, & Schattman, 1993; Giangreco & Meyer, 1988; Giangreco & Putnam, 1991; Hamre-Nietupski et al., 1989; Stainback & Stainback, 1990; Stainback & Stainback, 1992; Stainback et al., 1989; Thousand & Villa, 1989; Vandercook, York, & Forest, 1989; Villa, Thousand, Stainback, Stainback, 1992; Williams et al., 1986). Equally important is the emerging evidence that including students with significant disabilities in general education schools and classrooms can be beneficial for students without disabilities (Giangreco, Cloninger et al., 1991; Giangreco, Dennis et al., 1993; Giangreco, Edelman, Cloninger, & Dennis, 1993; Helmstetter, Peck, & Giangreco, 1993; Kishi, 1988; Peck, Carlson, Helmstetter, 1992; Peck et al., 1991; Putnam, Rynders, Johnson, & Johnson, 1989).

Providing special education services in general education environments will require a shift in how we think about educating diverse groups of students and how teachers operate. Special educators will no longer group students with special education needs together in isolated areas for instruction. General educators will no longer automatically refer students with differing needs out of the general classroom for support. Rather, general education teachers, special education teachers, related service providers, administrators, parents, students, and community members will work collaboratively to modify and adapt general education curricula, activities, and materials to meet the needs of diverse groups of students. When necessary, teams will identify supplemental curricula and develop ways of infusing them into general education class lessons and activities. We have only begun to discover the myriad of beneficial possibilities created when teams collaborate to teach diverse groups of students.

SECTION II

DESCRIPTION OF COACH

DESCRIPTION OF COACH

WHAT IS COACH?

COACH is an **assessment and planning tool** designed to identify the content of a student's educational program for implementation in general education settings and activities, based on individually determined valued life outcomes. COACH provides methods to:

1. Determine **family-centered learning priorities** using a structured process (i.e., Family Prioritization Interview, Parts 1.1–1.5).
2. Translate priorities into **annual goals** (Part 2.1).
3. Identify **learning outcomes beyond the top IEP priorities** to be targeted for instruction (Breadth of Curriculum, Part 2.2).
4. Identify **general supports** the student needs to have access to education and pursue individually determined valued life outcomes (Part 2.3).
5. Summarize the student's educational program components using the **Program-at-a-Glance** (Part 2.4).
6. Develop **short-term objectives** (Part 2.5).
7. Organize the **instructional planning team** and become familiar with the student and general education program (Parts 3.1–3.3).
8. Develop the **student's schedule** for general education classrooms and other inclusive settings that specifies identified learning outcomes and general supports (Part 3.4).
9. **Plan and adapt learning experiences to accommodate diverse groups** of students (Part 3.5).

COACH includes lists of **learning outcomes designed to extend or supplement, not replace, general education curricula** (Part 1). Each of the COACH learning outcome lists includes activities commonly occurring in daily life. These broadly stated activities are made up of clusters of skills that, when grouped together, allow a person to participate, at least partially, in typical settings with peers who do not have disabilities. Although there is some overlap depending on the age of the student, the learning outcomes listed in COACH contain many activities not typically included in the general education curriculum. Usually, most of the skills that make up these activities are mastered outside of academic environments (e.g., drinking by mouth, dressing, making choices), and therefore, typically are not included in general education curricula. The COACH listings are designed to be useful for students who have not mastered these skills prior to entering school or by the ages when children without disabilities have acquired the skills. Learning outcome lists are categorized as cross-environmental and environment-specific (see Figure 1).

Cross-environmnental lists refer to activities typically occurring across many environments. Cross-environmental lists included in COACH are those labeled Communication, Socialization, Personal Management, Leisure/Recreation, and Applied Academics. Activities within these lists (e.g., offering assistance to others, making requests, eating with utensils, reading) are used across many settings such as home, school, work, or a variety of community settings.

Motor (i.e., gross and fine), cognition, and sensory skills are three areas that cross many environments, yet are absent from the COACH listings. These three areas represent subskills embedded in all cross-environmental and environment-specific activities. For example, the motor subskill of grasping and the cognitive subskill of means/end only become useful when they are combined and applied with other skills, such as eating with utensils. A student with a visual impairment and motor disabilities may need to use a tactual searching skill to make a choice on a communication board. The purposeful omission of the motor, cognitive, and sensory areas as separate listings does not diminish their importance. On the contrary, the user of COACH should **consider how these skills**

15

CROSS-ENVIRONMENTAL

Communication

Socialization

Personal Management

Leisure/Recreation

Applied Academics

ENVIRONMENT-SPECIFIC

Home

School

Community

Vocational

Figure 1. Curricular areas in COACH.

Choosing Options and Accommodations for Children • © 1993 by Michael F. Giangreco • Baltimore: Brookes Publishing Co.

are applied to outcomes desired for a student and how those outcomes may contribute to pursuing valued life outcomes.

Environment-specific lists of outcomes refer to activities typically associated with use in specific environments. Environment-specific lists included in COACH are labeled Home, School, Community, and Vocational. For example, preparing breakfast, making a bed, and washing dishes are activities that usually occur at home. Participating in small group instruction and managing school-related belongings are done in school. Crossing an intersection and making a purchase are done in community settings. Interacting appropriately with coworkers, and using a time clock/sign-in are done at work.

Priorities

COACH is designed to help teams **identify the content of a student's individualized education program (IEP)**. COACH envisions that program as consisting of three major components. See Figure 2. The focal point of this content, as depicted by the inner circle in Figure 2, is a **small set of individual goals that represent the highest priorities for the student**. These learning priorities are determined by the parents and/or student using the Family Prioritization Interview (Parts 1.1–1.5); see Figure 3. Limiting the number of goals on a student's IEP is based on the belief that IEP goals should represent the **top priorities that a team can commit to teaching intensively** during the school year. Individualized education plans that attempt to document every detail of the educational program by including, for example, 35 goals and 140 objectives, spend more time consuming space in file cabinets than they do enhancing the education of students. Typically, educational teams cannot

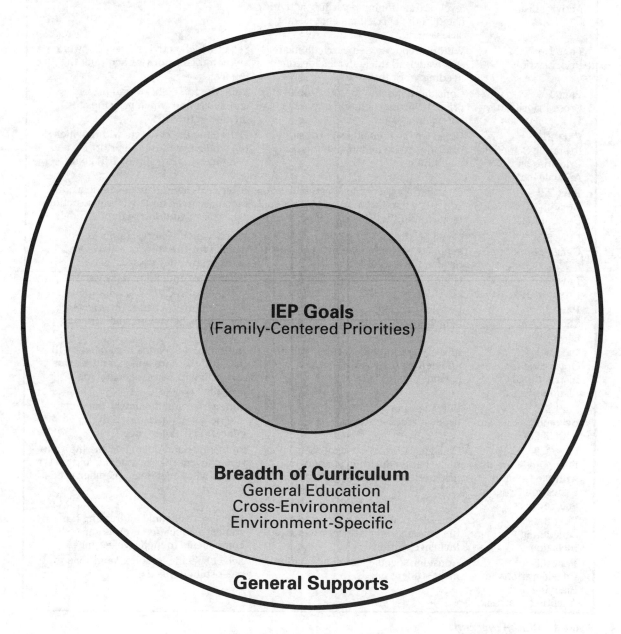

Figure 2. Educational program components.

Choosing Options and Accommodations for Children • © 1993 by Michael F. Giangreco • Baltimore: Brookes Publishing Co.

COACH OVERVIEW

Part of COACH	Divergent Aspect	Convergent Aspect
Part 1.1 Valued Life Outcomes	Gather information about the current status and desired future status of valued life outcomes to set a context for the rest of COACH.	Select one to three valued life outcomes that the family feels should be emphasized during the year as part of the school experience.
Part 1.2 Selecting Curricular Areas To Be Assessed	Consider all the curriculum areas in COACH to determine which areas need to be assessed in Part 1.	Select a subset of the curriculum areas in COACH to assess in Part 1, those that include potential priorities for this year.
Part 1.3 Activity Lists	Gather information on the student's level of functioning regarding activities listed in the curriculum areas being assessed.	Select activities needing work this year.
Part 1.4 Prioritization	Within each assessed curriculum area, reconsider all the activities identified needing work this year.	Select which activities needing work are potential priorities and rank the top five.
Part 1.5 Cross-Prioritization	Consider a maximum of the top five priorities from each of the assessed curriculum areas.	Rank the top eight overall priorities and determine which priorities to include in the IEP.
Part 2.1 Restating Selected Priorities as Annual Goals	Consider the contexts where the priorities to be included in the IEP might be used.	Determine the contexts within which the student will use the priorities and combine to write annual IEP goals.
Part 2.2 Breadth of Curriculum	Consider a variety of general education and other curricular areas for potential inclusion in the educational program.	Select curriculum areas and learning outcomes to be targeted for instruction this year in addition to the IEP goals.
Part 2.3 General Supports	Consider the variety of general supports/accommodations that may be needed for the student.	Select which general supports are needed for the student to have an appropriate education.
Part 2.4 Program-at-a-Glance	None	Summarize educational program components (Parts 2.1, 2.2, 2.3).
Part 2.5 Short-Term Objectives	Consider various conditions, behaviors, and criteria.	Write objectives based on selected conditions, behaviors, and criteria.
Part 3.1 Organizing the Instructional Planning Team	Identify the individuals who will be affected by team decisions, and consider possible tasks.	Determine which team members will make up the core and extended team and who will be responsible for identified tasks.
Part 3.2 Becoming Familiar with the Student	Consider a broad range of facts and needs about the student.	Summarize and document the facts and needs that pertain to the educational experience.
Part 3.3 Becoming Familiar with the General Education Program and Setting	Consider a broad range of facts about the general education curriculum, instructions, routines, and settings.	Summarize and document the information relevant for the student, and clarify what each team member needs to know.
Part 3.4 Scheduling for Inclusion	Consider possibilities for addressing the student's educational program in inclusive settings.	Develop a schedule addressing the student's educational program components in inclusive settings.
Part 3.5 Considerations for Planning and Adapting Learning	Consider specific lesson adaptations to meet student needs.	Select specific lesson adaptations to meet student needs.

Figure 3. COACH overview

Choosing Options and Accommodations for Children • © 1993 by Michael F. Giangreco • Baltimore: Brookes Publishing Co.

intensively address such quantities of goals with a sufficient level of quality. The focal priorities identified through COACH are addressed instructionally with students throughout the school year within the broad school context.

Breadth of Curriculum

Instruction that is limited to the small set of priorities generated using the Family Prioritization Interview could result in an unnecessarily narrow education for the student. **Family-centered priorities should be viewed as a focal subset of learning outcomes within the framework of a broader educational program.** COACH includes a process to identify **additional learning outcomes** beyond the top IEP priorities to be targeted for instruction. These are referred to as the **Breadth of Curriculum** and are depicted as the second circle in Figure 2. Breadth of Curriculum learning outcomes may include any combination of activities or skills from cross-environmental, environment-specific, or general education curricula. For example, parents of one child may identify a variety of socialization, communication, personal management, and community skills as instructional priorities for their son. The Breadth of Curriculum for this student may also include learning outcomes or instructional targets in curriculum areas such as reading, language arts, music, physical education, and math. Breadth of Curriculum learning outcomes are documented in less extensive ways than IEP goals and objectives, through methods used in general education classrooms (e.g., report cards, skill checklists, tests, narrative reports, portfolios of student work).

Not all Breadth of Curriculum learning outcomes are necessarily targeted for instruction across the entire school year. For example, a student's Breadth of Curriculum might include some general education learning outcomes in industrial arts. The industrial arts class may be offered in the second semester only; therefore, those learning outcomes would not be addressed until January. Other curriculum areas are taught throughout the entire school year. Breadth of Curriculum within these areas may be arranged in a sequence in which some learning outcomes are taught before others, or some learning outcomes may be targeted for instruction throughout the full year. Clarifying the initiation date for the Breadth of Curriculum learning outcomes and the expected duration of teaching will have an impact on the number of outcomes targeted for instruction and scheduling.

Breadth of Curriculum refers only to additional learning outcomes beyond the IEP goals and objectives and should not be confused with class locations where instruction occurs. One student might not have any general education curriculum goals in her program, yet receive all of her instruction in general education classes. For a different student there might be learning outcomes from several general education curriculum areas on which he will receive instruction across a variety of inclusive settings throughout the school day. In Part 3, examples demonstrate how a student's individual educational needs may be addressed in a class designed for a different curricular area (e.g., a student might pursue learning outcomes in communication and language arts through a science class).

As a rule, the general education curriculum is always the first consideration in selection of learning outcomes to be included in a student's Breadth of Curriculum. Too often, the general education curriculum is automatically excluded from a student's program if she has intensive special education needs. It is vital to augment or extend the curricular areas included in COACH, Part 1 with general education curricula to ensure that students have a broad-based school experience leading toward valued life outcomes (Part 1.1). School may also offer opportunities for incidental learning through exposure to new experiences; this is not specifically addressed in Breadth of Curriculum. While determining the Breadth of Curriculum may be useful across a range of educational placements, COACH is specifically geared toward students who are receiving special educational services (i.e., specially designed instruction) in chronological age–appropriate general education or other integrated settings (e.g., a community vocational setting).

The Breadth of Curriculum should be determined **soon after** the student's top priorities have been restated as annual goals. Determining the Breadth of Curriculum offers opportunities for team members to discuss similarities and differences regarding their ideas about the student's educational needs. Through this process, team members continually clarify and refine the shared framework necessary to extend collaborative efforts on behalf of the student. Although ensuring a Breadth of Curriculum for a student is part of a school's responsibility, it should be agreed to by **all team members including the family**, and be clearly documented. Documentation can help avoid conflicts caused by differing expectations among team members regarding what the student should learn.

General Supports

COACH also includes a method for identifying **general supports** that **need to be provided to or done for students** to allow them access to education throughout the school year (Part 2.3). General supports are depicted as the outer circle in Figure 2. Unlike learning outcomes (e.g., IEP goals, Breadth of Curriculum) which require a change in student behavior, general supports do not necessarily require learning by the student. Rather, general supports require changes in the behavior of those who interact with the student. General supports provide broad, cross-situational assistance; they are not as specific as learning adaptations, discussed in Part 3.5. General supports allow access to education and/or are needed for the student to achieve identified learning outcomes. Listed below are five major categories of need requiring general supports, and examples of each:

1. **Personal needs:** feeding, dressing, giving medication, tending to personal hygiene needs
2. **Physical needs**: passive range of motion, positioning and handling; providing mobility from place to place; managing special equipment such as braces, orthotics, wheelchairs; making environmental modifications; providing a student with postural drainage and/or suctioning prior to eating; clean intermittent catheterization; providing accessible transportation; arranging the physical environment so it is free of obstacles
3. **Sensory needs**: accommodating visual and/or hearing impairments by adjusting distance, location in space, background, lighting, volume; Braille translation; managing sensory aids such as hearing aids and glasses; sign language interpretation
4. **Teaching others about the student**: teaching staff and/or classmates how to use the student's augmentative communication system; explaining to teachers and peers the meaning of certain sounds or behaviors that the student uses; teaching seizure management protocols to staff; teaching crisis intervention protocols to staff
5. **Providing access and opportunities**: arranging an inclusive vocational experience; taking a student into town for community instruction; enrolling the student in extra-curricular activities; access to nonpunitive times and places in the school for a student to regain personal control

General supports may be provided by teachers, related service personnel, or other team members, including the family and student. Peers may appropriately provide some general supports. For example, after careful consideration for the privacy and dignity of the student with disabilities as well as the feelings of students without disabilities, it may be that, since they are in an excellent position to do so, a small group of students who were in class with the student with disabilities the previous year can explain to new students how this student communicates with his peers. Caution should be observed when involving peers in providing, or assisting with general supports to ensure that any such involvement is considered mutually beneficial and appropriate. What is considered appropriate likely will vary from place to place. Some general supports can be addressed in classrooms or other inclusive settings; others are addressed appropriately in private areas.

HOW DOES COACH FIT INTO AN OVERALL ASSESSMENT PLAN AND IEP DEVELOPMENT?

COACH is meant to be used as **one part of an overall approach** to planning an appropriate educational program for a student. COACH is not designed to determine eligibility for special education services, nor is it meant to provide a comprehensive assessment profile of a student. It is imperative that planning teams reach consensus regarding how COACH will fit into the overall preparation of the IEP. COACH assists in developing a number of IEP components, such as partial information about the student's present level of performance (additional assessment sources are likely to be necessary for a complete report on present level of performance); annual goals; short-term objectives; information about general supports; and extent of participation in general education. COACH should not be relied upon for classification, historical data, or the identification of alternative testing techniques. Although the results of COACH will be useful in determining the need for related services, COACH does not address how to make related services decisions. A companion process, VISTA (Vermont Interdependent Services Team Approach), builds on the results of COACH to assist teams in reaching consensus regarding the need for related services (Giangreco, 1990a, 1990b, in press a; Giangreco, Edelman, & Dennis, 1991).

The following chronology lists major events related to IEP development when COACH is used:

1. An evaluation team determines if the student is eligible for special education services.
2. A student planning team is formed.
3. The planning team decides to use COACH to assist in the development of the student's IEP.
4. The planning team decides what other assessments are needed to determine the student's present level of performance, strengths, and needs (e.g., occupational therapy, physical therapy, communication, reading). No goals or related services recommendations are generated based on these assessments. The team also collects any other pertinent reports, historical data, or existing assessment results.
5. A planning team member is selected to complete Part 1 of COACH with the family. Part 1 results in a short list of family-centered priorities to be restated as annual goals. In COACH Part 1.1, the family is encouraged to think about valued life outcomes from both the learning outcome and general supports perspectives. Parts 1.2 through 1.5 exclusively focus on identifying learning outcomes that are designed to pursue valued life outcomes.
6. The team uses Part 2 of COACH to develop annual goal statements based on family-centered priorities (Part 2.1), identify other learning outcomes to be targeted for instruction (Breadth of Curriculum, Part 2.2), and determine what general supports are needed for access to an appropriate education (Part 2.3).
7. Once the student's educational program components (Goals, Breadth of Curriculum, General Supports) have been identified, the team selects the most inclusive educational placement in which the student's educational program can be addressed. The first consideration should always be an age-appropriate, general educational placement in the school the student would attend if she did not have a disability. This placement refers to the age-appropriate grade to which the student is assigned, not the program content. It refers to the general placement (e.g., grade 3, grade 10), but does not necessarily specify the student's classroom or daily schedule of classes and activities.
8. Once the student's educational program components and placement have been determined, the team is in a position to determine the need for related services. Prior to this point, the team does not have sufficient information to make appropriate related services decisions that are educationally supportive and necessary (Giangreco et al., 1991). VISTA or other approaches can be used to explore the interrelationships among potential related services to ensure educational relevance and necessity, as well as to avoid undesirable gaps, overlaps, and contradictions in related services recommendations.
9. Once the need for and functions of related services have been determined and specifically referenced to the student's individually determined educational program components, the team can operate in subteams to develop short-term objectives and general support plans. This occurs **after** related services decisions have been made so the team knows which service providers will support each of the educational program components. In this way staff time can be used efficiently; only those members the team has determined need to be involved with a specific educational program component will devote time to planning for that component.
10. The team develops a schedule for the student by using a matrix to explore instructional activity possibilities. This involves comparing the student's IEP with the daily schedule in the general education classroom and other inclusive settings. The scheduling suggestions in COACH Part 3

are useful only for students who are placed in general education classes or are in transition to a general education setting.

11. The same subteams established to write short-term objectives and plans to accommodate general supports can develop lesson adaptation plans. These plans match the individual student's needs while maintaining the integrity of lessons for classmates without disabilities. Lesson adaptation plans integrate the input of the various subteam members and reflect ongoing team members' interactions (e.g., meetings, informal contacts, peer input).

Once a team has decided to use COACH, items 4 through 9 typically are completed within a few weeks. Frequently, items 4 through 9 are completed at the end of the school year in preparation for transition to a new class. COACH by itself does not address the myriad of transition planning issues for students. Therefore, COACH may be used as one part of a more comprehensive transition process. Timelines for transition planning will need to be determined individually. Then, items 10 and 11 are addressed at the beginning of the new school year. This sequence of events means that developing a quality IEP is not one event that takes place for half an hour on a scheduled day; rather, it is a process and sequence of logically ordered events dependent upon the events that precede them.

HOW DOES COACH ADDRESS PLANNING FOR A STUDENT'S EDUCATIONAL PROGRAM IN INCLUSIVE SETTINGS?

COACH is not designed to determine a student's educational placement, although the information it generates can be useful in making such decisions. The basic placement question is, "What is the most inclusive placement where the student's individually determined educational program components can be addressed given supplemental supports and aids if needed?" This means that the components of the student's educational program must be known **before** an informed placement decision can be made. A chronological age–appropriate general education placement in the school the student would attend if she did not have a disability should always be the first consideration. Unfortunately, many students have been automatically relegated to special classes and special schools without having the opportunity of being educated in inclusive settings. COACH can help teams with placement decisions and provide a process for evaluating the opportunities available for instruction in general education classes and other inclusive settings (Part 3.4). COACH can be a useful component of transition planning when students are being moved from self-contained to general education classes. Using COACH in combination with other exemplary practice based approaches will ensure that children with disabilities will almost never require placement in separate classes or schools.

What is meant by providing special education services in age-appropriate general education settings can be clarified by discussing the type of involvement a student may have in various class activities. Three options are presented here to indicate how a student could participate in general class activities. These options can occur in combination.

The first option is for the student to participate in the general class activity by pursuing the **same learning outcomes** as his classmates in basically the **same ways**. This option requires no significant changes in curriculum, instructional strategies, or resources.

The second option, **multi-level curriculum and instruction**, refers to identifying **different goals and objectives** for a diverse group of students **within the same curricular area** and teaching them within the **same lesson or activity** (Campbell, Campbell, Collicott, Perner, & Stone, 1988; Collicott, 1991; Giangreco & Putnam, 1991). This approach is not new to education, since it is an application of Bloom's (1956) Taxonomy of Educational Objectives, including: knowledge, comprehension, application, analysis, synthesis, and evaluation. For example, all the students may be in a reading lesson. The student with special needs is learning to identify (read) representations on a communication board (e.g., photos, symbols, words) while others are learning to read orally with appropriate pauses to match punctuation. Multi-level curriculum and instruction is already a common practice in many general education classrooms because the needs of nonlabeled students vary widely. It can be extended to include students with a wider range of abilities than typically is pursued within general education. For example, in a math lesson one student is applying computational skills to a word problem while another is learning to count with correspondence. Both students are pursuing math learning outcomes but at different levels within the same activity or lesson. Use of multi-level approaches is becoming increasingly prevalent in schools with the popularity of multi-graded classrooms.

The third option, **curriculum overlapping**, occurs when a diverse group of students is involved in the **same lesson**, but they are pursuing **goals and objectives from different curricular areas** (Giangreco & Meyer, 1988; Giangreco & Putnam, 1991). For example, students in science lab are learning about properties of electricity. A student with special needs may be involved in the science lab to learn the communication and socialization skills of following directions, accepting assistance from others, or engaging in a school job with a peer without disabilities. When curriculum overlapping takes place, the general class activity is used as a vehicle to teach other goals. This approach opens many opportunities for students to participate in classes previously considered inappropriate for them by some educators. Curriculum overlapping is part of the basis of our philosophy regarding placement. General education classes and other inclusive settings offer numerous untapped opportunities to address students' educational needs when teaching methods include active student participation.

Occasionally, no readily apparent opportunities may exist for the student to participate in a lesson or activity using multi-level or curriculum overlapping approaches. This may make it necessary for the student to engage in an alternative activity. For example, during a time when general education students are taking a half-hour paper and pencil test, it may be appropriate for a particular student to do individual work in the classroom. For regularly occurring times when an alternative might be appropriate, teams should consider the student's individual needs for community-based activities, such as pedestrian skills or purchasing, that might not be addressed adequately within the general class schedule. Decisions become more complex when students miss valuable classroom experiences to pursue alternative activities. This is when the team needs to evaluate whether or not the alternative activity is desirable enough to continue as a component of the student's educational program. Certain general supports are appropriately attended to in private (e.g., catheterization or postural drainage may be carried out in the health office). **Caution should be exercised when selecting alternative activities** since most student needs can be met in general education class situations given creative planning, a commitment to inclusion, collaboration among professionals and families, and the availability of active learning experiences. Within each option (e.g., same, multi-level, curriculum overlapping) it is recognized that some students will need individualized supports.

FOR WHOM SHOULD COACH BE USED?

COACH is designed for use with students ages 3–21 who are attending school and are identified as having moderate, severe, or profound disabilities. With modifications, components of COACH may be used with students who are younger or have lesser disabilities. COACH does not attempt to duplicate general education curricular areas appropriate for students with mild disabilities who may be pursuing much or all of the general education curriculum. Nor does it include many of the developmental skills frequently considered in working with infants and toddlers. Some people have successfully used COACH for younger children or those with mild disabilities by substituting other curricular listings of learning outcomes while retaining the COACH process steps. Blank forms included in Appendix B may be used for these purposes.

HOW LONG DOES IT TAKE TO COMPLETE COACH?

Since COACH is a flexible tool, completion time varies widely. **Part 1**, which culminates in the selection of family-centered priorities, **can be completed in approximately 1 hour**. Field-testing indicates that it takes closer to 1½ hours when both parents participate in the Family Prioritization

Interview or for first time users. The time required to use Parts 2 and 3 also is highly variable due to the numerous factors involved in writing annual goals, short-term objectives, schedules, lesson plans, and so forth. It is important to remember that the times indicated do not require the participation of all team members at the same time. For example, the 1 hour time commitment to complete Part 1 (Family Prioritization Interview) may affect only the parent and one other team member. The time it takes to complete COACH often decreases as team members become increasingly proficient in the use of COACH. Table 1 shows completion time approximations for Parts 1, 2, and 3.

WHO CAN FACILITATE COACH?

COACH Part 1 (Family Prioritization Interview) can be facilitated by any team member familiar with the process (e.g., special or general education teacher, psychologist, occupational therapist, communication specialist, physical therapist, family support personnel). The planning team should reach consensus regarding who will assume this responsibility. COACH can be facilitated by a person familiar with the student and family (to enhance individualization of the tool) or by a neutral party who is naive to the dynamics of the situation and therefore can minimize bias during question-asking. Debate exists about which of these approaches is preferable. A person familiar with the family and student must guard against asking questions to elicit parent responses that reflect the interviewer's own opinions. A person unfamiliar with the family must be able quickly to adapt questioning style, vocabulary, pacing, and so forth.

Teams are encouraged to enter into the COACH process ONLY if group members are willing to accept and use the priorities generated by the family. After identifying family priorities for inclusion on the IEP, not accepting those priorities or failure to follow through on them (e.g., not including negotiated priorities as goals on the IEP or adding a series of your own goals to those of the family) likely will harm, rather than facilitate, family-school collaboration. Parts 2 and 3 offer ample opportunities for professional input and can be completed by any combination of members designated by the team.

WHO SHOULD BE INVOLVED IN COMPLETING COACH?

In addition to the individual designated by the team to facilitate COACH **Part 1 (Family Prioritization Interview), the parents and/or the student are the only other required participants**. Every effort should be made to include the student whenever possible and appropriate. Additional team members, peers, siblings, and others may be invited on a negotiated basis with the student and parents. These additional people are not required to attend because the purpose of Part 1 is to identify the individual's and/or family's priorities.

As the student becomes a young adult there may be a conflict between what the student wants as a priority and what the parents want. In such cases, prior to the beginning of the interview, it

Table 1.   Completion times for COACH

Part	Time range in minutes
Introducing COACH to Participants	5–10
Part 1.1 Valued Life Outcomes	10–15
Part 1.2 Selecting Curricular Areas To Be Assessed	5–10
Part 1.3 Activity Lists	15–25
Part 1.4 Prioritization	13–15
Part 1.5 Cross-Prioritization	12–15
ALL OF PART 1	60–90
ALL OF PART 2[a]	60–90
ALL OF PART 3[a]	60–90

[a]Scheduling changes and lesson adaptations require ongoing evaluation and adjustment.

should be clarified who will be in charge of these decisions. As a general rule of thumb, we suggest that students be extended the same rights and responsibilities offered to peers without disabilities (e.g., high school students have a significant role in determining their course of study).

The first page of the COACH forms includes spaces to document that the results of Part 1 were shared with team members not in attendance during the interview. Users of COACH are cautioned that **the presence of too many people at the Family Prioritization Interview can interfere** with desired parent participation, therefore individual judgment should be used. Parts 2 and 3 require the involvement of all or some of the team members, depending upon tasks, time, and interests as negotiated by the team. These parts of COACH offer alternatives to supplement face-to-face interactions and therefore address the ongoing problem of limited time availability.

WHERE AND WHEN SHOULD COACH BE COMPLETED?

The place and time to complete Part 1 (Family Prioritization Interview) should be **individually negotiated with the family to maximize their opportunity for participation**. Therefore, Part 1 can be done at any convenient time and at any mutually agreed upon location. The family home and the school are the two most common locations. Parts 2 and 3 also may be completed anywhere, although school is the most common location. Parts 2 and 3 are frequently completed using a combination of team and subteam meetings, telephone calls, and mail.

WHEN DURING THE SCHOOL YEAR SHOULD COACH BE COMPLETED?

COACH has been used successfully during the intake process for new students regardless of time of year. For those students already in the school system, a number of schools have found it beneficial to complete Parts 1 and 2 in the spring in preparation for the coming school year. Part 3 then may be completed at the beginning of the new school year. This allows more refined and ongoing planning to take place at the times and in the settings where learning will occur. Regardless of when during the school year COACH is used, it should be considered one part of a more comprehensive assessment and planning process.

HOW CAN WE EVALUATE THE EFFECTIVENESS
OF EDUCATIONAL PROGRAMS BASED ON COACH?

Evaluation of program effectiveness and quality has incorporated the use of various approaches such as coded or anecdotal observations, reports of staff, permanent products, and videotapes of work samples. Teams may evaluate: 1) student progress toward goals and objectives; 2) the impact of teaching methods on valued life outcomes; 3) the quality of inclusive lesson plans with respect to learning outcomes for all students being taught; 4) members' progress toward completing team designated tasks; and 5) the impact of the education plan on team members such as the family, teachers, paraprofessionals, and related service providers.

Evaluation data are meant to guide team decision-making regarding the student's educational program. It is crucial that adjustments to the educational program be based upon a variety of considerations, such as student progress toward objectives and provision of general supports; expanding inclusive opportunities; enhancing perceptions by peers of the individual; encouraging a positive impact on students without disabilities; promoting positive self-concept; advancing positive social interactions; promoting the physical and/or emotional health of students; or increasing the appropriate choice-making capacity the learner can exercise upon her environment. Ongoing evaluation should extend beyond narrowly defined instructional objectives to assess changes in the quality of students' lives (Meyer & Janney, 1989).

While COACH holds great potential for pursuing valued life outcomes, it is successful only if such pursuits are realized for the student and family. A two-tiered process should be used to evaluate students' educational programs to examine explicitly the activities and outcomes of the schooling experience as related to a student's valued life outcomes. The first tier explores the current status of the student's progress toward identified learning outcomes and the effects of general supports provided to the student. The second tier identifies how the student's valued life outcomes have changed based on what the student learned and what supports were provided to him.

For example, a student with severe disabilities may have a goal to improve his eating skills (e.g., chewing, swallowing, amount of food intake). This goal may have been selected as a priority of the family because the child has such a difficult time eating that he is frequently undernourished and underhydrated. The physician has said that if this does not change soon the child will need a gastrostomy tube for feeding. Additionally, problems with swallowing occasionally result in the aspiration of food, leading to respiratory infections. At the first tier of evaluation, the student's food intake skills would be evaluated. If the student's eating skills have improved, that is not enough to claim success. Data collected may show a change, but is that change significant? The second tier would consider whether those changes have resulted in improvement of the corresponding valued life outcome, in this case, improved health as determined by a decrease in aspiration-related illness, weight gain, improved nutrition, and vitality as reported by the family. Family and peer feedback is essential in considering whether the valued life outcome has improved. This form of social validation has long been discussed (Evans & Meyer, 1987; Meyer & Janney, 1989; Voeltz & Evans, 1983; Wolf, 1978), although less frequently acted upon. An evaluation approach such as this fundamentally changes what constitutes success in an educational program. Development of a valued life outcome-referenced evaluation process is consistent with family-centered perspectives; current exemplary practices (Fox & Williams, 1991a); and the intention of COACH to increase the probability that students' lives will improve as a result of being educated in inclusive settings.

SECTION III

DIRECTIONS FOR USING COACH

Part 1

Directions
for Completing the
Family
Prioritization
Interview
(Parts 1.1 – 1.5)

> Consumers are reminded that COACH is a flexible tool. Its process is specifically intended to help teams develop educational plans that reflect valued life outcomes identified by the family and to encourage participation in a variety of inclusive settings. Your team is encouraged to modify COACH as necessary to be useful under unique circumstances.

The directions for completing COACH are illustrated below in the example of Tommy S. Additional examples for students of different ages with varying characteristics appear in Appendices D and E.

DESCRIPTION OF TOMMY S.

Tommy S. is an 8-year-old boy who lives with his parents and younger sister. He responds to the presence and interactions of people, especially other children, by changing his facial expressions and eye movements. He likes to eat pizza, spaghetti, fruit, and ice cream and needs to have his food cut up in small pieces and fed to him. The people who spend time with Tommy believe that he understands much of what is said to him. He communicates primarily through his facial expressions as well as by vocalizations like crying and laughing. Tommy moves from place to place by others pushing him in his wheelchair. He likes being in places where there is much activity. Tommy has limited use of his arms and needs at least partial assistance with most activities of daily living. He can hear and see, but it is unclear how well these senses are functioning because his responsiveness to sights and sounds is inconsistent. Tommy enjoys music, rough-housing, going outside, and his pet dog Danish. He is an avid Buffalo Bills football fan. Tommy receives special education support services from an inclusion facilitator, paraprofessional, occupational therapist, physical therapist, speech-language pathologist, and vision specialist in a grade 3 class in his neighborhood school.

PREPARATION FOR COACH, PART 1

1. **Select a student** for whom COACH is an appropriate tool in educational planning.
2. All team members are encouraged to **read** the COACH manual and **understand** its content. The family may wish to review Part 1 of COACH in advance. While this is certainly acceptable, encourage parents to avoid the temptation of preparing or filling in the forms on their own. **COACH is not designed to be used as a questionnaire to be filled out by the family in isolation; its value is in the interaction between the family and a designee of the team.**
3. Discuss the use of COACH for the student as a team, including the family, and **make a team decision about using it**.
4. The team verifies that by entering into the COACH process they **agree to accept and act upon the educational priorities identified by the family and/or the student**. This is done by agreement to generate a single set of discipline-free goals based on the results of Part 1 (Family Prioritization Interview).
5. Decide, as a team, how the use of COACH fits into the **overall assessment and planning** process for the student.
6. Determine **who should complete COACH (Part 1)**. Involve the family in making this decision.
7. Determine **if anyone else should be present** during the completion of Part 1 in addition to the interviewer and the family. Some teams have found it helpful to use another person to record additional notes or fill in the COACH forms. Others facilitating COACH prefer to record and facilitate the interview simultaneously.
8. **Schedule a date, time, and location** for the interview that is mutually agreeable between the family and interviewer.
9. **Prepare the forms** that will be used to conduct Part 1 (Family Prioritization Interview). Copy the forms you will need from the manual; most are found in Appendix B. This will allow you to

have the manual open to the directions so you can refer to them and also have the forms displayed in front of the family, thus avoiding the awkward flipping of pages back and forth between the forms and directions. You also may wish to copy Figure 1 (page 16), Figure 2 (page 17), and Figure 3 (page 18), as well as Appendix A (Scoring Key and list of Valued Life Outcomes).

10. **Be familiar with the directions and content of COACH before** attempting to complete Part 1. You still may need to refer to the directions until you become comfortable with the tool. If this is one of the first times you are using COACH or you have not received feedback in a while, you are encouraged to ask a team member to observe you conducting the Family Prioritization Interview and **to use the Self-Monitoring and Peer Coaching Guide to COACH** (Appendix C).

11. **Complete the cover page** of COACH (Part 1) by writing the identifying information (e.g., name, date, educational placement, team membership) **prior** to the Family Prioritization Interview. Do not take the family's time to fill in this information. At this point the only blank column will be the one on the right side of the page labeled "Date reviewed." You will notice that the cover page does not include historical data, diagnosis, classification, IQ, type of disability, or any other similar information frequently found on cover pages of other assessment tools. This information is absent simply because it is not relevant to the task of identifying family-centered learning priorities for the student. (See Figure 4.)

INTRODUCTION TO THE FAMILY PRIORITIZATION INTERVIEW, PART 1

The following steps must be attended to **before any questions are asked** in Part 1.

1. **Review the "Introduction to Part, the Family Prioritization Interview."** (See Figure 5.) This guide is also included in the set of blank forms in Appendix B. It is important to share this information so the family knows what to expect during the Family Prioritization Interview. Typically, this introduction is completed in approximately 5 minutes.

2. Have Figure 1 (Curricular Areas in COACH), Figure 2 (Educational Program Components), Figure 3 (COACH Overview), and Appendix A (Scoring Key and list of Valued Life Outcomes) available throughout the Family Prioritization Interview to refer to as necessary. Some teams have found it helpful to show the family a Program-at-a-Glance (see Figure 17, page 64) so they can see an end product as an example of where the process is heading.

3. Position yourself close enough to the family that they can see the forms as you fill them out. Typically, the interviewer **sits next to, or between, the parents and/or student**. Use a single copy of the COACH forms during the interview so participants are focused on the same material at the same time. If the parents are nonreaders or nonreaders of English, adjust your interview style so they are not dependent on looking at written materials. COACH has been used successfully with parents and students who are nonreaders, by skillful individualization. Respect the families' cultural and individual variations in, for example, eye contact, the level of formality, and vocabulary.

4. The skillfulness of the person facilitating COACH is a crucial variable to a successful interview. Maintain a **quick pace** and request **short answers**; however, quick need not mean rushed. Keep the interview focused on the content, and politely redirect participants from tangents and storytelling. Storytelling may be important at another time. Tools such as MAPS (the McGill Action Planning System) may facilitate learning about the student through personal stories (Vandercook et al., 1989). More in-depth discussions occur later in COACH (Parts 2 and 3) on those activities the family selects as priorities. Engage in **active listening**, and move from question to question without much pause between. By keeping within the suggested time parameters you can increase the likelihood parents will have enough energy left during Part 1.5 to bring the process to closure.

PART 1.1. VALUED LIFE OUTCOMES

1. **Review "Information to Share with the Family"** found at the top of the Part 1.1 form. (See Figure 6.) Participants must be aware that the purpose of Part 1.1 is to set a context for the

CHOOSING OPTIONS AND ACCOMMODATIONS FOR CHILDREN

COACH

Student's name __Tommy Smith__ Date of birth __1-7-83__

Date of Family Prioritization Interview (COACH, Part 1) __4-10-91__

Person interviewing the family __M. Giangreco__

Educational placement(s) __Grade 3 class at Spring Street Elementary School with Special Education Supports__

PURPOSE AND DIRECTIONS: In the spaces provided write the names of all team members and their relationship to the student. The "Date reviewed" column is used to indicate the date the results of COACH are shared and reviewed with each team member. It is neither desirable nor necessary for all team members to participate in the completion of COACH (Part 1). Therefore the "Date of Family Prioritization Interview (COACH, Part 1)" will be different from the "Date reviewed" for team members who were not present. This review provides a method for documenting the exchange of important educational information among all team members.

Name of team member	Relationship to student	Date reviewed
Martha Smith	Mother	
David Smith	Father	
Peggy Green	Grade 3 Teacher	
Lisa Jones	Special Ed. Support Teacher	
Jim Kent	Speech-Language Path.	
Karen Drake	Occupational Therapist	
Angela Ramirez	Physical Therapist	
Fred Banker	Vision Specialist	
Tom Billford	Paraprofessional (Aide)	

Figure 4. Cover page of COACH.

PART 1
FAMILY PRIORITIZATION INTERVIEW
INTRODUCTION

The following headings represent categories of information and sample statements to be shared with participants. YOU ARE ENCOURAGED TO INDIVIDUALIZE THE INFORMATION TO FIT EACH FAMILY YOU INTERVIEW. Figures 1, 2, and 3 can be used to illustrate some points.

PURPOSE OF THE FAMILY PRIORITIZATION INTERVIEW

"The purpose of this meeting is to identify the top learning priorities for [student's name] that you [parent] believe would improve [his/her] life. We will also determine which of the selected priorities you feel should be included on the IEP."

"We have asked you [parent] to participate in this meeting because we recognize that you have an important role to play in determining educational priorities for [student's name]."

CONTENT

"The areas we will explore in today's meeting are meant to extend or augment general education curricula. COACH includes a variety of curriculum areas that are designed to improve [student's name] valued life outcomes." See Figure 1.

EXPLAIN WHAT IS GOING TO HAPPEN

TIME

"Today's meeting will take approximately 1 hour" (to complete Parts 1.1–1.5).

RATE

"During that hour, I will be asking you a variety of questions. Since there are so many areas to consider, I want you to be aware that I will be presenting questions rather quickly and will ask for relatively short answers from you."

PARENT OPPORTUNITIES TO DISCUSS PRIORITIES IN DEPTH

"Since some of the questions I ask you will be more important than others, I will ask you to go through each area rather quickly so that we can focus on what you think is important. Once we know what you think is important, then we can plan to spend more time discussing those areas in greater detail <u>after</u> we complete Part 1 or at another time."

OUTCOMES

"By the end of today's meeting you will have selected what you believe are the top priorities for [student's name] to improve [his/her] valued life outcomes. We will discuss and decide which of these priorities should be included on the IEP."

RELATIONSHIP OF PRIORITIES TO THE REST OF THE SCHOOL PROGRAM

"While focusing on [student's name] top educational priorities is important, these priorities represent only one part of the educational program. We realize that [student's name] also needs to have a broad school experience. This will be addressed in Part 2 where we will consider other learning outcomes to be taught (Breadth of Curriculum) and general supports needed to improve [student's name] valued life outcomes." See Figures 2 and 3.

NEXT STEPS

"After today's meeting, we will review your priorities with other team members who were not here today. Once each member is aware of the priorities, we will develop goals, objectives, and the classroom schedule of activities."

Figure 5. Introduction to the Family Prioritization Interview, Part 1.

subsequent parts of COACH. Part 1.1 explores the family's perceptions about valued life outcomes for their child. A sample is available in Figure 6.

2. **Ask questions 1–11**; note that question 7 is only for students 13 years old or older. Record brief answers in the spaces provided. Let the family know they need not answer any questions they find too sensitive. Although you may ask the questions as written, it is desirable to reword them to match the individual situation.

3. After the questions have been asked and answers recorded, ask the parents, "Which of the outcomes do you feel should be emphasized during this school year? Please pick a maximum of three." This is a convergent step. While all of the valued life outcomes may be important, have the family **select one to three outcomes they feel are most important to emphasize this year**. Put a check mark in the corresponding boxes to show which outcomes should be emphasized.

PART 1.2. SELECTING CURRICULUM AREAS TO BE ASSESSED

1. **"PART 1.2" is printed at the top of each activity list** (e.g., Communication, Socialization, Vocational). See Figure 7 for the Communication example.

2. Explain to the family that the purpose of Part 1 is to determine a *small* set of family-centered educational priorities, rather than all the learning outcomes to be included in the student's educational program. Therefore, it is **not necessary to assess all the curricular areas** listed in COACH during Part 1; opportunities for that will be available in Part 2. Part 1.2 encourages the family to **consider the nine curriculum areas** in COACH that are designed to augment or extend the general education curriculum. Tell the family they will be **asked to select the areas they wish to assess** in Part 1. Typically, families select four to six areas. While any number of areas (one to nine) can be selected, remember **this is a point in the process where you are narrowing the focus** in an attempt to identify priorities.

3. **Show the family the first activity list** (start with Communication), so they can see the types of items included under that heading. Inform the family that although the Communication activity list addresses a variety of valued life outcomes, it most strongly addresses outcome #4 (Having a level of personal choice and control that matches one's age). Relating the activity list to the family selections in Part 1.1 (Valued Life Outcomes) may help them decide whether they wish to assess this area. For example, if parents said they wanted to emphasize developing social networks for their child, refer them to the Socialization activity list, which is heavily weighted toward that outcome.

4. Give the family one of three options. They appear at the top of the activity list form. First, they may choose to **"ASSESS IN PART 1."** By doing so they are **indicating that the list includes potential learning priorities for this school year**. Second, they may choose to **"ASSESS IN PART 2."** This means the activity list may **include some important content that should be part of the student's Breadth of Curriculum**, but probably is not a priority from their perspective. Checking this box eliminates the area from assessment during Part 1 and defers it until Part 2. This option gives some parents the security of knowing that certain items will not be lost in the shuffle. It will be difficult for parents to select Breadth of Curriculum unless the interviewer has done a thorough job explaining the concept during the Introduction. Third, they may choose to **"SKIP FOR NOW."** Checking this box eliminates the area from assessment in Part 1. Although this does not eliminate the area from consideration during Part 2, it indicates that the **family does not consider this a vital area of emphasis this year**. Parents who select "SKIP FOR NOW" typically have one of three motivations: First, the youngster may be very **proficient** in the area and, therefore, it may not need attention. Second, the parents may feel that the activities addressed on the listing are **beyond what the student could reasonably be expected to pursue during the coming year**. Third, the parents may feel that improving the student's valued life outcomes in a particular area would be **addressed through general supports** (Part 2.3) rather than through the attainment of learning outcomes. For example, in the Personal Management area, the family may view many of the activities as those that others must learn to do for

INFORMATION TO SHARE WITH THE FAMILY: An underlying assumption of COACH is that students' lives should be better as result of being in school. **The purpose of Part 1.1 is to provide a context so the subsequent parts of COACH can be directly related to valued life outcomes.** The following list shows five valued life outcomes that have been identified by families whose children have disabilities:

1.   Having a Safe, Stable Home in Which To Live
2.   Having Access to a Variety of Places and Engaging in Meaningful Activities
3.   Having a Social Network of Personally Meaningful Relationships
4.   Having a Level of Personal Choice and Control that Matches One's Age
5.   Being Safe and Healthy

The following questions obtain information about the student's current and desired future status related to the valued life outcomes. These questions set a context for subsequent parts of COACH, and are not to generate in-depth discussion. After this information is collected, the family is asked to indicate which valued life outcomes they wish to have emphasized in the school program during the coming year. Therefore, spend only 10–15 minutes having the family briefly answer the questions. **Reword the questions** to match the individual situation. A summary of the family's responses is recorded in the spaces provided.

#1: HAVING A SAFE, STABLE HOME IN WHICH TO LIVE

1.   Where does [student's name] live currently (e.g., at home with family, foster home, community residence)?

 At home with parents and younger sister

 (NOTE: Since this information may already be known, you can record the answer and restate it to the family: "OK, we know that [student's name] lives with you and his sister"; then move on to question 2.)

2.   If everything goes as you hope, do you anticipate that [student's name] will continue to live where [she/he] is throughout the school years?

 Yes

 If not, what would be a desirable place?

 —

3.   Would you like to talk about what a desirable place would be for [student's name] to live as an adult, or is that too far in the future to discuss at this time?

 Too far in future

 If yes, where?

 Maybe an apartment with a roommate

4.   Is there any place you would like to avoid having [student's name] live in the future?

 Avoid any institution or other large facilities (e.g., nursing home, large group home).

(continued)

Choosing Options and Accommodations for Children • © 1993 by Michael F. Giangreco • Baltimore: Brookes Publishing Co.

Figure 6.   Part 1.1: Valued life outcomes.

36

Figure 6. (*continued*)

PART 1.1   VALUED LIFE OUTCOMES
(*continued*)

#2: HAVING ACCESS TO A VARIETY OF PLACES AND ENGAGING IN MEANINGFUL ACTIVITIES

5. Where does [student's name] go, and what kinds of activities does [he/she] do that [he/she] likes or make [him/her] feel good about [himself/herself]? Does [student's name] go where the family goes, following the family routine? *Goes to the park, likes to swing, swimming, music, rough-housing, playing with his dog, watching softball games, watching the Buffalo Bills on TV*

6. Would you like to see these places and/or activities change or expand in the near future? If so, how? *He follows the family routine and is pretty active; would like to see activities expand that he could do on his own and do with peers rather than adults.*

7. ASK THIS QUESTION ONLY IF THE STUDENT IS 13 YEARS OLD OR OLDER. Have you given any thought to what kinds of activities [student's name] might do or places [he/she] might go as a young adult? For example, in the future how might [student's name] spend [his/her] time that is now spent in school (e.g., competitive work, supported work, volunteering, continuing education?) *NA (too young)*

#3: HAVING A SOCIAL NETWORK OF PERSONALLY MEANINGFUL RELATIONSHIPS

8. Besides [his/her] family, whom does [student's name] have friendships or personal relationships with (e.g., relatives, classmates, friends)? *A couple kids in the neighborhood; cousins; a girl from church (Sarah); classmates, but only in school*

9. Would you like to see these relationships change or expand in the near future, and if so, how? *Expand friendships in and out of school.*

(*continued*)

Figure 6. (*continued*)

PART 1.1   VALUED LIFE OUTCOMES
(*continued*)

#4: HAVING A LEVEL OF PERSONAL CHOICE AND CONTROL THAT MATCHES ONE'S AGE

10. What, if anything, would you like to see change in [student's name] current level of personal choice and control that would enable [him/her] to pursue a more enjoyable life? <u>More</u> <u>choices; it seems like everybody always decides things for him.</u>

#5: BEING SAFE AND HEALTHY

11. What, if anything, would you like to see change in [student's name] current health or safety that would enable [him/her] to pursue a more enjoyable life? <u>Chronic respiratory</u> <u>infections — maybe from aspirating foods; need to get</u> <u>more fluids in him</u>

WHICH OUTCOMES SHOULD BE EMPHASIZED?

Now, ask the family, "Which of the outcomes do you feel should be emphasized during this school year? Although all of the outcomes may be important, please pick a maximum of three." **Put a check in the appropriate space in the right-hand column.**

#1: Having a Safe, Stable Home in Which To Live	Emphasize this Year? _____

#2: Having Access to a Variety of Places and Engaging in Meaningful Activities	Emphasize this Year? _____

#3: Having a Social Network of Personally Meaningful Relationships	Emphasize this Year? ✓

#4: Having a Level of Personal Choice and Control that Matches One's Age	Emphasize this Year? ✓

#5: Being Safe and Healthy	Emphasize this Year? ✓

COMMUNICATION[a]

COACH

PART 1.2

Check only one box:
ASSESS IN PART 1 (Potential Priorities this Year) ☒ ASSESS IN PART 2 (Breadth of Curriculum) ☐ SKIP FOR NOW ☐

#	ACTIVITIES	SCORE	PART 1.3 NEEDS WORK	PART 1.4 POTENTIAL PRIORITY	PART 1.4 RANK	PART 2.2 BREADTH OF CURR.
1	Indicates Continuation or Expresses More (e.g., makes sound or movement when desired interaction stops to indicate he or she would like eating, playing, and so forth to continue).		N Y			
2	Makes Choices when Presented with Options.		N Y			
3	Makes Requests (e.g., for objects, food, inter-actions, activities, assistance).		N Y			
4	Summons Others (e.g., has an acceptable way to call others to him or her).		N Y			
5	Expresses Rejection/Refusal (e.g., indi-cates when he or she wants something to stop or does not want something to begin).		N Y			
6	Greets Others.		N Y			
7	Follows Instructions (e.g., simple, one-step, or multi-step directions).		N Y			
8	Describes Events, Objects, Interactions, and so forth (e.g., uses vocabulary, nouns, verbs, adjectives).		N Y			
9	Responds to Questions (e.g., if asked a question he or she will attempt to answer).		N Y			
10	Asks Questions of Others.		N Y			
11	Sustains Communication with Others (e.g., takes turns, maintains attention, stays on topic, perseveres).		N Y			
			N Y			
			N Y			

Comments:

Scoring Key: R = Resistant to the assistance of others   P = Partial skill (25%–80%)   Use scores alone
E = Early/emerging skills (1%–25%)   S = Skillful (80%–100%)   or in combination.

[a]Communication may be exhibited or received in any combination of ways (e.g., speaking, gestures, signing, keyboards).

Figure 7. Part 1.2: Selecting Curriculum Areas to be assessed.

the student, such as learning to dress him, assisting him with drinking, and attending to his bowel/bladder needs. **Check only one of the three boxes reflecting the family choice.**

5. **DO NOT COMPLETE ANY OTHER INFORMATION ON THE COMMUNICATION PAGE AT THIS POINT. COMPLETE PART 1.2 ON EACH PAGE FOR THE NINE ACTIVITY LISTS BEFORE COMPLETING PART 1.3 ON ANY PAGE.**

6. **Repeat the steps listed above by checking one of the three boxes on each of the nine activity lists.** The following offers additional information that can be shared with families regarding each curriculum area listed in COACH. Each curriculum area includes activities referenced to a variety of valued life outcomes; some areas emphasize certain outcomes over others.

Curriculum Area	Valued Life Outcomes Emphasized and Other Information
Communication	#4: Having a Level of Personal Choice and Control that Matches One's Age
Socialization	#3: Having a Social Network of Personally Meaningful Relationships
Personal Management	#4: Having a Level of Personal Choice and Control that Matches One's Age
	#5: Being Safe and Healthy
Leisure/Recreation	#2: Having Access to a Variety of Places and Engaging in Meaningful Activities
	#4: Having a Level of Personal Choice and Control that Matches One's Age
Applied Academics	#2: Having Access to a Variety of Places and Engaging in Meaningful Activities
	#4: Having a Level of Personal Choice and Control that Matches One's Age
	Note: This area may have limited application for preschoolers.
Home	#1, #2, #3, #4, and #5, with no particular emphasis on any single outcome.
School	#2: Having Access to a Variety of Places and Engaging in Meaningful Activities
	#3: Having a Social Network of Personally Meaningful Relationships
	#4: Having a Level of Personal Choice and Control that Matches One's Age
Community	#2: Having Access to a Variety of Places and Engaging in Meaningful Activities
	#4: Having a Level of Personal Choice and Control that Matches One's Age
	Note: These activities may be most appropriate for older students.
Vocational	#2: Having Access to a Variety of Places and Engaging in Meaningful Activities
	#4: Having a Level of Personal Choice and Control that Matches One's Age
	Note: This area includes only two items for students in elementary and middle school.

PART 1.3. ACTIVITY LISTS

1. **Be familiar** with the content of the activity lists. Verify, rather than ask, questions that have obvious answers (e.g., very basic communication items such as Expresses More or Makes Choices, for a student who is verbal). At the other end of the spectrum, you may group together items that logically are prerequisites. For example, if you ask a parent about the child's ability to count with correspondence and learn that the child has no concept of numbers, then it is not necessary to ask about higher level math items (e.g., computation, measurement).

2. **Complete Part 1.3 only for activity lists checked "ASSESS IN PART 1." (See Figure 8.)**

3. Remind the family that this section will be **presented quickly** and that **brief answers** are requested. **DO NOT SPEND TOO LONG ON ANY SINGLE ITEM.**

4. **Individualize the presentation and wording of each item to match the situation.** The activity lists can give you a starting point or may be used verbatim.

5. When presenting items, remind and encourage participants to think broadly about the activity by considering such aspects as: increasing tolerance to the activity; developing core skills; using alternative/augmentative modes to engage in the activity; preparation, initiation or termination of the activity; tempo/rate and duration; self-monitoring; social/communicative aspects of the activity; retention over time; generalization across people, settings, cues, or materials; quality; expansion of repertoire; problem-solving regarding the activity; or assisting others.

6. For each listed activity, ask the family to rate the student's current level of functioning. Using the interview format, **ask** about the activity, **listen** to the response, **select the score(s)** that you believe reflects the response, **verify** the score by sharing it with the parents, and **record** the score. Record a score using the codes found at the bottom of each Activity List and in Appendix A. Score an item as **E** for "Early/emerging Skills;" **P** for "Partial Skill;" or **S** for "Skillful." Scoring should focus on what the student *can* do. Score an **R** for "Resistant to the assistance of others" in combination with E, P, or S as appropriate. Scores may be recorded singularly (e.g., E; P; S), or in any combination (e.g., R-E; P-S; R-S). **Do not spend a great deal of time discussing minor discrepancies in scoring.** This score represents the family's perception of the student's functioning level; therefore, consistency with professional estimates is not necessarily expected.

7. **Before scoring another activity on the list, ask the family, "Does the student 'NEED WORK' on the activity this year?"** Circle **"Y"** for "YES" if the student needs work on the item **this year** or **"N"** for "NO" if the student does not need work on the item this year. Remind the parents that circling "N" is typically done for one of three reasons: 1) the student is perceived to be sufficiently proficient with the activity given her age, 2) the family feels that pursuit of the identified activity is beyond what they consider reasonable during the coming year, or 3) the family believes that the identified activity is best addressed through general supports provided to the student by others. This step is meant to narrow further the focus toward the selection of priorities. The question at this point is *not* whether a listed activity is a priority, but whether it **needs work this year**. Parents should be encouraged **not to** indicate YES (Y) for every item because this does not help narrow the focus. The number of items marked "Y" or "N" may vary widely for different students.

8. **Repeat the two previous steps,** scoring the activity and indicating whether it needs work, for each activity on the list.

9. Once all the items on a list are scored and the "Needs Work" section is completed, ask if anyone present at the interview would like to **add any items** to this curriculum area. If so, write items in the blank spaces, and score these items using the same procedures as for the previous items.

10. **Write any pertinent comments** in the space provided at the bottom of the page. It is useful to code comments with the activity number to which they refer.

11. **Repeat steps (1–10) for each activity list that was marked "ASSESS IN PART 1."** *COMPLETE PART 1.3 ON EACH OF THE SELECTED ACTIVITY LISTS BEFORE COMPLETING PART 1.4.*

COMMUNICATION[a]

PART 1.2

Check only one box:
ASSESS IN PART 1 (Potential Priorities this Year) ☒ ASSESS IN PART 2 (Breadth of Curriculum) ☐ SKIP FOR NOW ☐

#	ACTIVITIES	PART 1.3 SCORE	NEEDS WORK	PART 1.4 POTENTIAL PRIORITY	RANK	PART 2.2 BREADTH OF CURR.
1	Indicates Continuation or Expresses More (e.g., makes sound or movement when desired interaction stops to indicate he or she would like eating, playing, and so forth to continue).	S	N (Y)			
2	Makes Choices when Presented with Options.	P	N (Y)			
3	Makes Requests (e.g., for objects, food, interactions, activities, assistance).	E	N (Y)			
4	Summons Others (e.g., has an acceptable way to call others to him or her).	E	N (Y)			
5	Expresses Rejection/Refusal (e.g., indicates when he or she wants something to stop or does not want something to begin).	S	(N) Y			
6	Greets Others.	P	N (Y)			
7	Follows Instructions (e.g., simple, one-step, or multi-step directions).	E	N (Y)			
8	Describes Events, Objects, Interactions, and so forth (e.g., uses vocabulary, nouns, verbs, adjectives).	E	N (Y)			
9	Responds to Questions (e.g., if asked a question he or she will attempt to answer).	E	(N) Y			
10	Asks Questions of Others.	E	(N) Y			
11	Sustains Communication with Others (e.g., takes turns, maintains attention, stays on topic, perseveres).	E	(N) Y			
			N Y			
			N Y			

Comments: Tommy has no consistent way to communicate that is easily understood by people other than his family.

Scoring   R = Resistant to the assistance of others   P = Partial skill (25%–80%)   Use scores alone
Key: E = Early/emerging skills (1%–25%)   S = Skillful (80%–100%)   or in combination.

[a]Communication may be exhibited or received in any combination of ways (e.g., speaking, gestures, signing, keyboards).

Choosing Options and Accommodations for Children • © 1993 by Michael F. Giangreco • Baltimore: Brookes Publishing Co.

Figure 8.   Part 1.3: Activity List.

PART 1.4   PRIORITIZATION

1. After Part 1.3 has been completed for each area marked "ASSESS IN PART 1," **Part 1.4 is to be completed on those areas only.** See Figure 9.
2. Participants are reminded that the **purpose of Part 1.4 is to focus further on the family's top priorities.**
3. Now **return to the first area that was assessed in Part 1.3.** At this point, the interviewer tells those present (e.g., family, professionals, advocates) that they will be given opportunities to offer input regarding which chosen activities are potential priorities. Inform all participants that Part 1.4 **does not include discussion** about the potential priorities; any potential priorities for the student will be recorded and **judgment will be deferred.**
4. The interviewer asks participants to **consider a variety of criteria** when considering whether an item is a **potential priority for this year.** Most important, they are encouraged to think about how an activity relates to improving the valued life outcomes the family selected at the end of Part 1.1. Additionally, the interviewer asks participants to consider criteria such as the practicality of the activity, its usefulness in the future, the immediacy of need, the frequency of its use, and whether it *builds on the student's strengths and interests.* Inform participants they will ultimately be selecting a maximum of five activities from each list they assessed.
5. First, the family is asked to consider each activity on a list (e.g., Communication) for which "Y" (Yes, Needs Work) was circled. The interviewer places a check mark in the column marked **"POTENTIAL PRIORITY"** for each activity the parents feel are **potential priorities for this year.** Participants are informed that this stage of the process is designed to help narrow the number of activities being considered; participants are encouraged to **select a subset of these activities** that need work. After the parents have indicated which YES **activities** are potential priorities, other team members present at the interview may add their ideas and opinions; this input would be recorded in the same way, with a check mark in the corresponding box under POTENTIAL PRIORITY. If team members suggest items not selected by the parents, the interviewer should make it clear to the parents that these additional items are offered for their consideration and that ultimately they have no obligation to select these items.
6. The **family is then asked to rank the top five activities** on the list marked as potential priorities, using number 1 for the highest priority, number 2 for the next highest priority, and so forth. If two or more priorities are equal or close in rank they may both be ranked with the same number. It is important for participants to understand that **only the top five ranked priorities will be used at the next, and final level of prioritization.** Therefore, the most important consideration is ranking the top five priorities. If the family is able to select the top five priorities but is having difficulty ranking them, do not spend time struggling over rank order, merely ask the family if it is acceptable to put the top five in any order. If participants are having difficulty selecting top priorities, it is sometimes helpful to eliminate activities that parents know are not on the top five. Do not spend time considering whether a particular activity should be ranked 8 or 9. Typically this would be a waste of time because neither will advance to the next level. It is conceivable that a particular assessed area may include no potential priorities.
7. **Repeat the prioritization process for each assessed curriculum area.**

PART 1.5   CROSS-PRIORITIZATION

1. **Transfer the top five priorities** from each assessed area to the Cross-Prioritization grid in their ranked order. **Abbreviations may be used.** Some areas on the Cross-Prioritization grid may be marked "NOT ASSESSED;" others may be marked "ASSESSED, NO PRIORITIES." See Figure 10.
2. **Review the "INFORMATION TO SHARE WITH THE FAMILY"** located in the middle of the Cross-Prioritization grid.
3. Considering the same criteria as used in prioritization (e.g., referenced to valued life outcomes, frequency, strength of the student, immediacy of need), **the family is asked to give an overall**

COMMUNICATION[a]

PART 1.2

Check only one box:
ASSESS IN PART 1 (Potential Priorities this Year) ☒   ASSESS IN PART 2 (Breadth of Curriculum) ☐   SKIP FOR NOW ☐

#	ACTIVITIES	PART 1.3 SCORE	NEEDS WORK	PART 1.4 POTENTIAL PRIORITY	RANK	PART 2.2 BREADTH OF CURR.
1	Indicates Continuation or Expresses More (e.g., makes sound or movement when desired interaction stops to indicate he or she would like eating, playing, and so forth to continue).	S	N (Y)	✓	2	
2	Makes Choices when Presented with Options.	P	N (Y)	✓	1	
3	Makes Requests (e.g., for objects, food, inter-actions, activities, assistance).	E	N (Y)			
4	Summons Others (e.g., has an acceptable way to call others to him or her).	E	N (Y)	✓	3	
5	Expresses Rejection/Refusal (e.g., indi-cates when he or she wants something to stop or does not want something to begin).	S	(N) Y			
6	Greets Others.	P	N (Y)	✓	4	
7	Follows Instructions (e.g., simple, one-step, or multi-step directions).	E	N (Y)			
8	Describes Events, Objects, Interactions, and so forth (e.g., uses vocabulary, nouns, verbs, adjectives).	E	N (Y)			
9	Responds to Questions (e.g., if asked a question he or she will attempt to answer).	E	(N) Y			
10	Asks Questions of Others.	E	(N) Y			
11	Sustains Communication with Others (e.g., takes turns, maintains attention, stays on topic, perseveres).	E	(N) Y			
			N Y			
			N Y			

Comments: Tommy has no consistent way to communicate that is easily understood by people other than his family.

Scoring   R = Resistant to the assistance of others   P = Partial skill (25%–80%)   Use scores alone
Key: E = Early/emerging skills (1%–25%)   S = Skillful (80%–100%)   or in combination.

[a]Communication may be exhibited or received in any combination of ways (e.g., speaking, gestures, signing, keyboards).

Figure 9.   Part 1.4: Prioritization.

PART 1.5   CROSS-PRIORITIZATION

Transfer a maximum of the top five priorities from each assessed area in their ranked order.

#	Communication	Socialization	Personal Management	Leisure/ Recreation	Applied Academics
1	Makes choices	Sustain interactions	Drinks/Eats by mouth		
2	Indicates more	Initiates interactions	Gives self ID Info	NOT ASSESSED	NOT ASSESSED
3	Summons others		Mobile within buildings		
4	Greets others				
5					

#	Home	School	Community	Vocational	Other ( )
1		Works at task indepen.		School jobs with peers	
2		Participates in small groups			
3	NOT ASSESSED	Participates in large groups	NOT ASSESSED		NOT ASSESSED
4					
5					

INFORMATION TO SHARE WITH THE FAMILY: First, the family will be asked to rank a maximum of the top eight overall. **Second,** the interviewer verifies the reason for the selection of the priority and assigns a number corresponding to a valued life outcome. **Third,** the family is asked to verify that their selections accurately reflect their priorities. **Fourth,** the participants negotiate which of the ranked priorities should be restated as annual goals and be "Included in the IEP," which should be considered for inclusion as part of the "Breadth of Curriculum," or which should be primarily a "Home" responsibility. **Fifth,** the interviewer will explain how the results of Part 1 will be used and what comes next.

Rank	OVERALL PRIORITIES	Write # Valued Life Outcomes	Included in the IEP	Breadth of Curriculum	Home
1	Drinks and eats by mouth	5			✓
2	Indicates more	4	✓		
3	Makes choices when presented with options	4	✓		
4	Sustains interaction with peers	3	✓		
5	Participates in small and large groups	2+3		✓	
6	Summons others	3+4	✓		
7	Works at task independently	4	✓		
8	Mobile within buildings	4		✓	

Choosing Options and Accommodations for Children • © 1993 by Michael F. Giangreco • Baltimore: Brookes Publishing Co.

Figure 10.   Part 1.5: Cross-Prioritization.

ranking for a maximum of the top eight priorities for the coming year. The priorities are listed in the spaces provided under the heading OVERALL PRIORITIES. Some families find themselves weary of "ranking" by this point. Remind families that what is most important is that a priority be included on the OVERALL PRIORITIES list. The order of overall ranking is not crucial. Therefore, do not spend a lot of time, for example, determining if an activity should be ranked 2 or 3; just record both on the OVERALL PRIORITIES list.

4. After the family has ranked a maximum of their top eight overall priorities, the person facilitating COACH verifies the intent of the priorities and clarifies how they are referenced to the valued life outcomes. The purpose of this step is to ensure that the family and interviewer share the same understanding of why each activity was identified as a priority. The person facilitating COACH starts with the first ranked priority and offers her understanding of the rationale for the family's selection. For example, the person facilitating COACH might say, "I want to make sure I understand your priorities. Please tell me if I am accurately summarizing your views that led you to select these priorities. Drinking and eating by mouth was your top priority for Tommy. I understand that this is because you are concerned that he does not eat and drink enough to maintain his health and that he aspirates food into his lungs which causes chest infections. Is that correct?" Once the family verifies or clarifies their view, a number corresponding to the valued life outcome(s) addressed by the ranked priority is recorded in the first column to the right of the ranked priority. These numbers (1–5) come from Part 1.1 (Valued Life Outcomes). Refer to Appendix A. In this case "5" (Being Safe and Healthy) would be recorded in the space next to the first overall priority as shown in Figure 10. This verification process is repeated for each of the overall priorities.

   This step is important because families often select the same activities for priorities but for different reasons. For example, one parent might identify COACH item number 24, Eats and Drinks by Mouth, as an overall priority for their child. This parent might indicate selecting this as a priority to improve the child's health since the child is prone to being undernourished and dehydrated because of his eating and drinking difficulties. A different parent might select the same priority for their child but for a very different reason. This second parent's child might eat well enough to be healthy, but the quality of the eating causes a negative social reaction from people who are near where the child is being fed. The parent feels that social interactions with peers who do not have disabilities will be enhanced if mealtime is somewhat neater; in such a case this activity would be coded "3" for Having a Social Network of Personally Meaningful Relationships. In both cases, why the activity was selected as a priority is completely individualized from the family's perspective. By knowing why the family wants to pursue a certain priority, the team can increase the probability that their planning, especially the writing of short-term objectives, will be relevant and match the family intentions.

5. The family is asked to **review their rankings** and make any changes to reflect more accurately their priorities or reasons for selection. The interviewer receives verification from the parents that the ranked priorities represent the most important learning outcomes for the student during the coming year.

6. Once the top eight priorities have been verified, the family is asked to make a final decision about the priorities and reach agreement with the interviewer about how each priority should be addressed, that is: **Included in the IEP**, or included in **Breadth of Curriculum**, or primarily a **Home** responsibility. Making this type of distinction will assist both in writing annual goals and in scheduling, as described in Part 3. By determining which option will be pursued for each priority, the team clarifies the extent of instructional emphasis for each priority. The three options are shown at the bottom right corner of the Cross-Prioritization grid. They are described below.

   Included in the IEP means the participants want this priority translated to attainable annual goals and short-term objectives. Inclusion on the IEP means the team agrees to focus intensively on this priority as part of the school program. Progress reporting and other forms of documentation will be used to monitor student progress and adjust instruction. The number of priorities translated into annual goals should be reasonable according to the characteristics of the child.

Breadth of Curriculum means this activity should be considered in Part 2 as a potential learning outcome to be targeted for instruction. If Breadth of Curriculum is selected, the priority will **not be translated into an IEP goal** and objectives but will be documented in a less extensive way. *Some teams have included a summary of the Breadth of Curriculum as an addendum to the IEP.* The main reasons people code a priority as Breadth of Curriculum are: 1) the family feels comfortable that this priority will be attended to through the school program and does not feel that it is essential to document on the IEP, and 2) the priority represents a new, exploratory area for the student's learning. For example, it may be a priority for Tommy to be mobile. The team wants to explore mobility options (e.g., motorized wheelchair), but none of the team members is sure whether it will be successful. Coding this priority as Breadth of Curriculum allows the team to target mobility for instruction while freely exploring possibilities. **Remember, a priority that is an IEP goal for one student may be included in Breadth of Curriculum for another.**

Home means the family wishes to take primary responsibility for teaching their child a particular activity. For example, the family may have selected toothbrushing as a priority because it effects the child's health and interactions with other children. The family may indicate they will take the lead on this at home. This does not preclude school support. For example, the team members may still decide it is desirable to practice toothbrushing after lunch as a support to the family but will not emphasize this activity. In some cases, parents who provide many community experiences for their child may ask the school to emphasize other areas of instruction and let the family teach community skills. This allows each family the opportunity to decide which learning outcomes to address. **Check only one of the three boxes for each ranked priority.**

7. **Review the final decisions** with the family by confirming which priorities will be translated into IEP goals. When using COACH, the family-centered priorities generated in Part 1.5 represent the only annual goals to be included on the student's IEP; other learning outcomes targeted for instruction may be included in the Breadth of Curriculum. When using COACH it would be **inconsistent to write an IEP based on the family-centered priorities and then add a series of additional annual goals based on professional perspectives unless further discussions and negotiations took place.** The interviewer might say, "I'd like you to take a look at your selections one last time. According to what you have shared with us, Tommy's IEP would include goals that reflect his five priorities. This means there would be approximately five annual goals on his IEP; it could vary slightly if it makes sense for some priorities to be combined or separated. Eating and Drinking will be primarily a home responsibility. Summoning Others and Mobility will be addressed in Part 2 (Breadth of Curriculum). Is this OK with you? Do you have any questions? I will share this information with the other team members who were not with us today. Next, we will translate these priorities into annual goal statements to review with you and other team members. We also need to begin working on the Breadth of Curriculum and general supports. I will be contacting you to discuss this further. We need to get a full picture of Tommy's program so we can figure out what educational and related services he might need. If you have questions feel free to call me."

8. Provide the family with a choice of having a copy of either the Cross-Prioritization grid as a summary of final decisions or all COACH forms.

9. Review the results of Part 1.1–1.5 with all team members listed on the cover page (Figure 4).

10. Make plans to complete Part 2 (writing annual goals, determining Breadth of Curriculum, identifying general supports, writing short-term objectives).

SUBSEQUENT ADMINISTRATIONS OF PARTS 1.1–1.5

When COACH is used for the first time with a student, each Part of the tool offers potentially valuable information to assist with decision-making. If COACH is used annually to develop IEPs, readministering each subpart of Part 1 with the family may be redundant. The following guidelines can assist with individually determining how best to approach readministration with a particular family:

1. Involve the family and other team members in deciding which sections of Part 1 need to be: a) readministered completely, b) administered in a modified fashion, or c) simply verified.
2. Teams may arrange to do the complete COACH to coincide with the 3-year evaluation. Complete use of COACH Part 1 (1.1–1.5) is recommended at least once every 3 years and can be done completely on a more frequent basis if desired by the team. Typically, COACH would not be done more than once per year. Some people have used the COACH process to develop multi-year plans (e.g., 3-year) rather than annual plans.
3. If earlier versions of COACH were used, it is recommended that you use COACH in its entirety because of the substantial changes in this version.
4. The responses to the questions in Part 1.1 (Valued Life Outcomes) may remain relatively unchanged over the course of 1 year; therefore,they could be quickly reviewed and verified with the family. The last subpart of Part 1.1 (identifying which valued life outcomes to emphasize during the school year) will be important to review regardless of how little the answers to the questions change. Part 1.2 (Selection of Curricular Areas) may be reviewed and curricular areas added or deleted. The decision whether to redo or verify Part 1.3 (Activity Lists) will depend upon the student's degree of progress. Regardless of whether previous subdivisions are redone or verified, it is advisable to redo Parts 1.4 and 1.5 (Prioritization and Cross-Prioritization). This will allow the family to adjust their priorities. Any readministration must be tailored to match the family situation.

Part 2

Directions for Defining the Educational Program Components

PART 2.1 RESTATING SELECTED PRIORITIES AS ANNUAL GOALS

If IEP goals are designed to guide the instructional program, then these goals must be written in such a way as to offer direction to the team who will implement the plan. This is particularly important if school teams develop annual goals in the spring to be used the following fall. When one team writes a goal for a student that ends up being used by a different team because of staff turnover or student placement changes, the intention behind the goal selection may be misunderstood. For example, if someone wrote the goal, "In community stores, Tommy will improve his ability to make purchases," one might assume that the focus of this goal was the acquisition of the core skills associated with purchasing (e.g., locating merchandise and paying for it). In reality, different students may each have a different focus related to purchasing. One student may need to learn problem-solving strategies for what to do when he cannot find an item; another may need to expand her repertoire of purchasing. For example, she knows how to buy prepackaged merchandise from shelves but may not know the skills needed in the bulk food section of the grocery store or the deli counter. Therefore, for each generally stated activity in COACH, the focus for short-term objectives could be one of many aspects (e.g., increasing tolerance, accepting/providing assistance, initiation, preparation, quality, tempo, rate, duration, self-monitoring, safety, problem-solving, termination, expansion of repertoire, communicative aspects, social-behavior aspects, retention over time, indication of choices/preferences, generalization). By clarifying the intent of a generally stated annual goal, the writers provide a direction to continue refined assessment and a focus for instructional planning.

Since the scope of an annual goal should be such that the learner can attain it within 1 year, the goal statements vary depending on the characteristics of the learner. For some students, the activities listed in COACH will represent appropriate annual goals, for others they may be too broad or too narrow. If the activities are too narrow for annual goals, two or more related activities may be combined into a single annual goal. In this case, COACH activities may serve as the basis for short-term objectives. If it is expected that the activities from COACH are too broad for the student to attain in a year, the goal statement is modified to reflect that, and short-term objectives are developed that describe milestones or progressive steps to achieving the goal. The annual goal statement should reflect an activity-based outcome for the student. If annual goals are shifted from activities to skills by the team, this may detract from focusing on the necessary clusters of behavior that constitute those activities.

It is suggested that priority annual goals include two main components: **context** (e.g., school, home, community, vocational site, settings with peers without disabilities, combinations, and so forth), and a **learner behavior.** The Annual Goal Worksheet (Part 2.1) is provided to assist you, if needed, in preparing annual goals. See Figure 11.

Context is important because it directs the users of the IEP to the ultimate settings and situations in which the student must function and encourages planning to be outcome oriented. It also provides a documented rationale for participation in inclusive environments. This can provide justification for transportation and other logistical components of implementing appropriate educational experiences in inclusive school and community settings.

Drafting annual goals does not necessarily require all team members to be present simultaneously. Once the priorities identified for the IEP (Part 1.5) are verified and agreed to by all team members, the team can negotiate various methods to translate them into written goal statements. While this can be completed as a group activity, it is often difficult to arrange meetings with the entire team. As an alternative, a member or members of the team can be designated to draft the goal statements for later refinement and verification by the full team. Such refinement and verification can occur face-to-face, over the telephone, or through correspondence. Goals are broken down into short-term objectives (Part 2.5) after being written in general statements, as discussed here.

Steps to Writing Annual Goals

1. Determine if it makes sense to combine any of the priorities to be included in the IEP. For example, for a particular student, Initiating Social Interactions and Greeting Others might be the same

PART 2.1 ANNUAL GOAL WORKSHEET
(Use as needed.)

Goal # _1_ (Rank # _2_ from Part 1.5)

Behavior _Indicates More_

Context _At school in typical settings like the playground_

Team Member Suggestions _Include cafeteria_

Final Goal Statement _Tommy will indicate that he wants more of something (e.g., food, drink, play) in a variety of school settings_

Goal # _2_ (Rank # _3_ from Part 1.5) _(e.g., cafeteria, playground, classroom)_

Behavior _Make choices when presented with options_

Context _Inclusive school Settings_

Team Member Suggestions _List settings (e.g., recess, lunch)_

Final Goal Statement _Tommy will make choices when presented with options in a variety of school settings (e.g. cafeteria, playground, classroom)_

Goal # _3_ (Rank # _4_ from Part 1.5)

Behavior _Sustains Interactions_

Context _Typical settings with peers without disabilities_

Team Member Suggestions _Small groups_

Final Goal Statement _Tommy will increase the time he sustains interactions with peers without disabilities in small group activities_

Goal # _4_ (Rank # _6_ from Part 1.5)

Behavior _Summons Others_

Context _When he wants someone who is not there_

Team Member Suggestions _—_

Final Goal Statement _Tommy will improve his ability to summon a person to him in situations in which he is separated from someone with whom he wants to interact._

Goal # _5_ (Rank # _7_ from Part 1.5)

Behavior _Works at task independently_

Context _Nonfrustrational task_

Team Member Suggestions _Increase length of time_

Final Goal Statement _Tommy will increase the length of time he can work at a task independently in situations in which he is presented with a task he is able to do (e.g., play with toy, class job)_

Figure 11. Part 2.1: Annual Goal Worksheet.

thing and can logically be combined into one goal (e.g., In school and community settings Carly will initiate interactions with peers by greeting them.). For other students, this may not make sense if Initiating Social Interactions refers to asking a friend to play a game, or inviting a friend to go to the movies, or striking up a conversation. In some instances it may be appropriate to write more than one annual goal for a single priority.

2. In the space provided on the Annual Goal Worksheet, write the behavior you want the student to use. *The behavior should match the intent of the priority and be attainable in 1 year.*

3. In the spaces provided on the Annual Goal Worksheet, write the context(s) in which the student will use the behavior. This encourages the team to assess, implement, and evaluate the student's progress toward the behavior in relevant settings rather than through isolated experiences.

4. Via either face-to-face, written, or other interactions, record team members' suggestions for changing the goals before they are finalized. Get this input from **all appropriate** team members before the goals are finalized.

Examples of Annual Goals

Examples based on Tommy's Cross-Prioritization (Part 1.5) include:

1. Tommy will indicate he wants more of something (e.g., food, drink, play, human interaction) in a variety of school settings (e.g., cafeteria, playground, classroom).
2. Tommy will make choices when presented with options in a variety of school settings (e.g., cafeteria, playground, classroom).
3. Tommy will increase the time he sustains interactions with peers without disabilities in group activities.
4. Tommy will improve his ability to summon a person to him in situations in which he is separated from someone with whom he wants to interact.
5. Tommy will increase the length of time he can work at a task independently in situations in which he is presented with a task he is able to do (e.g., play with a toy using his microswitch, do a class job).

NOTE: All of Tommy's priorities come from cross-environmental curriculum areas. It is not unusual for families to select many or all priorities from cross-environmental curriculum areas, especially for younger children.

Examples of Annual Goals for Other Students

1. Lorenzo will initiate social interactions with peers in general education classes, cafeteria, recess, and extra-curricular activities.
2. Molly will request basic wants and needs (e.g., food, drink, play, human interaction) in a variety of settings (home, school, and community).
3. Larena will be mobile between her homeroom and other classrooms.
4. Gerry will engage in cooperative leisure activities in physical education class and extra-curricular activities.
5. Jose will improve his ability to read braille at home, in school, and in the community.
6. Jai will react to touch from others by orienting toward the person and changing his facial expression when approached by peers or adults.
7. Astrid will tactually search her lap tray to locate and choose her next activity during recess.
8. Juanita will select appropriate clothing to wear to school.
9. Yvonne will increase her participation in large group activities in general education classes with peers who do not have disabilities.
10. James will eat meals at a socially appropriate rate in community restaurants.
11. Moira will improve her ability to terminate social interactions appropriately (e.g., conversations, table games) in the break room at her community vocational site.

PART 2.2   DETERMINING THE BREADTH OF CURRICULUM

Preparation for COACH Part 2.2, Breadth of Curriculum

1. Parts 1.1–1.5 (Family Prioritization Interview) of COACH must be completed prior to the team determining the Breadth of Curriculum. All team members must be aware of the results of Part 1.
2. Part 2.1 of COACH (annual goals) should be at least in a draft form. Having a clear understanding of the intent behind the selection of the top priorities to be included in the IEP can avoid overlap with the Breadth of Curriculum as well as facilitate integration of potential goals and activities.
3. Team members involved in determining the Breadth of Curriculum must **be familiar with the content of the general education curriculum** pertaining to the grade level in which the student will be placed. **It is necessary to have a list of grade-level learning outcomes available so team members may refer to them during their decision-making.** The grade level here does not necessarily refer to the student's functioning level, but rather the grade level class he is placed in or that is being planned for. Typically, general education class placements for students with intensive educational challenges closely match the student's chronological age (give or take 2 years). For example, an 11-year-old boy functioning at a pre-K level academically may still receive his education in a grade 5 classroom. General education content may be reflected in sources as course objectives, scope and sequence listings, skills checklists, or other documents describing the learning outcomes for students without disabilities at that grade level. A written copy of the learning outcomes from the various general education curriculum areas should be available to team members, including the family. **If the student for whom you are planning is likely to pursue some general education learning outcomes at grade levels other than where he is placed, those lists of learning outcomes should also be available to team members.**
4. Decide what approach the team will use to determine the Breadth of Curriculum. Although this can be accomplished at a large group team meeting, this method often presents logistical constraints. One option is to have the Breadth of Curriculum initiated by the core team, a teacher, or any other ad hoc group formed for this purpose. Then this initial work can be reviewed with other team members through face-to-face interactions, telephone calls, or by mail to reach consensus. The important task here is for the team to agree on how they wish to ensure team member input within reasonable time and logistical constraints. Team members participating in determining the Breadth of Curriculum **should be familiar enough with the student's characteristics, needs, interests, and level of functioning** to offer thoughtful input to the process.

How To Complete the Breadth of Curriculum Worksheet, Part 2.2

1. Fill in the blanks at the top of the page to indicate the student's name, grade being planned for, and the approximate number of available instructional hours/periods per day; this is meant to serve as a reminder to participants regarding time resources. See Figure 12; circled numbers refer to order of steps to completion.
2. In the spaces provided in the left column under the heading, GENERAL EDUCATION CURRICULUM, **write the grade level placement being planned for and list the general education curriculum areas available to students without disabilities** at that grade level. This list will vary from school to school as well as across age levels. Preschool teachers might list curriculum areas such as communication/language, play, social/emotional skills, and fine/gross motor skills. Elementary school teachers might list areas such as reading/language arts, math, science, art, physical education, music, computer, and social studies. High school teams may list areas such as science, math, social studies, and English, or they may be more specific (e.g., biology, geometry, Asian studies, creative writing) if such information is available. Other secondary level general education curricula might include areas like foreign language, industrial arts, home economics, health, physical education, vocational studies, and computer science.
3. Have the basic **content of each general education curricular area available** (e.g., district curriculum, list of grade-level learning outcomes). Also, have the listings of curricular activities

PART 2.2 BREADTH OF CURRICULUM WORKSHEET

① **Student name** _Tommy Smith_   **Grade being planning for** _3_

Approximate number of available instructional hours/periods per day = _5½ hours_

Curriculum Areas To Consider	④ How many of the **learning outcomes** in each curriculum area are potentially appropriate for student instruction this school year? (Check appropriate boxes.)				⑤ Target To Teach? ("+" or "−") see criteria	⑥ Source of Curriculum for Target Areas (e.g., general education scope and sequences, COACH activity item numbers)
	MOST (80%–100%)	SOME (20%–80%)	FEW (<20%)	MULTI-LEVEL		
② GENERAL EDUCATION CURRICULUM, GRADE _3_						Burlington Curriculum Guide (BCG)
③ Language Arts				K	−	
Math				K	−	
Science				K	−	
Social Studies				K	−	
Music				K	−	
Physical Educ.				K	+	BCG 20,67,94
Health				K	+	BCG 5,10,23
Computer				K	+	BCG C2,P5
Art				K	−	

CROSS-ENVIRONMENTAL CURRICULUM Communication[a]		✓			+	COACH 3,7
Socialization[a]		✓			+	COACH 20
Personal Management			✓		−	—
Recreation/Leisure		✓			+	COACH 38
Applied Academics[a]		✓			+	COACH 39,41
Other						

ENVIRONMENT-SPECIFIC CURRICULUM Home			✓		−	—
School		✓			+	COACH 60,65
Community			✓		−	—
Vocational[a]	✓				+	COACH 75

[a]Likely overlap with some portion of general education curriculum.

(#) = order in which steps of this worksheet are completed.

Choosing Options and Accommodations for Children • © 1993 by Michael F. Giangreco • Baltimore: Brookes Publishing Co.

Figure 12. Part 2.2: Breadth of Curriculum Worksheet.

from COACH Part 1.3 available. To avoid unnecessary paperwork, keep in mind the purpose of this part is to identify learning outcomes to be targeted for instruction. For secondary students it is not necessary to review every science curriculum, every math curriculum, or every social studies curriculum. Start with the grade placement curriculum and work from there. Sometimes verifying, for example, that a student is not expected to pursue certain learning outcomes (e.g., algebra) is important. Conflicts arise when teachers, families, and other team members do not share the same expectations about what the student is to learn and do in school. This step focuses team members on reaching consensus regarding expectations.

4. **Review each listed curriculum area** (i.e., general education, cross-environmental, environment-specific) and **put a check mark in one of the four boxes** in response to the question, "How many of the learning outcomes in each curriculum area are potentially appropriate for student instruction this year (the year being planned for)?" This is a fact-finding step; at this point **judgment should be deferred** regarding whether the curriculum area will be targeted for instruction or which specific learning outcomes will be targeted for instruction.

   a. Check **MOST** if approximately 80%–100% of the grade-level learning outcomes are appropriate for instruction given the student's individual needs and level of functioning. Since the focus of this Part is on learning outcomes, you are encouraged to consider any adaptations that may be required. General Supports will be addressed in Part 2.3; lesson adaptation considerations will be addressed in Part 3.5.

   b. Check **SOME** if approximately 20%–80% of the grade-level learning outcomes are appropriate for instruction given the student's individual needs and level of functioning.

   c. Check **FEW** if less than approximately 20% of the grade-level learning outcomes are appropriate for instruction given the student's individual needs and level of functioning.

   d. Check **MULTI-LEVEL** *if learning outcomes in this curriculum area may be appropriate but at a grade-level significantly different from that of peers.* What constitutes "significantly different" will be determined individually since service delivery variations such as multi-grade classes and individual class variations may differ. For example, it is possible that for a specific student with intensive special education challenges, FEW grade 10 science learning outcomes may be appropriate for instruction this year. Yet other science learning outcomes, at a different grade level, may be appropriate for instruction (e.g., 3rd-grade learning outcomes). In such a case, checking the box for Multi-level, and noting grade 3 does not suggest a grade 3 placement; it refers exclusively to learning outcomes. This option is called multi-level because the identified learning outcomes can be addressed through multi-level instruction (Collicott, 1991).

5. Once the fact-finding has been completed as described above, a decision must be made regarding **which curriculum areas should be targeted for instruction** (not merely exposure to the curricular content) and **which specific learning outcomes** in each selected area should be included in the student's program. **Put a " + " in the boxes that correspond to curriculum areas that will be targeted for instruction this year. Put a " – " in the boxes that correspond to curriculum areas that need not be targeted for instruction this year.** See Figure 12. The following are some basic criteria to consider when making this decision:

   a. **Are any curriculum areas state or district requirements?** For example, physical education and/or health education are requirements in many states or districts, regardless of whether the student has a disability label or not. These requirements and/or any other similar requirements should be targeted for instruction. If a required area is targeted for instruction the specific learning outcomes may still be individually determined and do not necessarily need to match the grade-level of the placement.

   b. **Do the curricular areas targeted offer a broad educational experience that improves the student's valued life outcomes?** If learning outcomes from a particular area are not targeted for instruction, this does not preclude the possibility of the student being in class where that curricular content is the focus for the majority of the class. For example, if art learning outcomes are not targeted for instruction, the student may still be placed in an art class and participate in art activities as a vehicle to address identified valued life outcomes, including educational learning outcomes, from other curriculum areas.

c. **Are the number of curricular areas targeted for instruction reasonable given the amount of available instructional time?** During the fact-finding step it is conceivable that there were learning outcomes identified as appropriate in many or all listed curriculum areas. While some curriculum content (e.g., communication or social skills) can be embedded within a variety of activities, team members often are faced with making some decisions to deal with the fact that there is more to be taught than time permits. The team must remember that they have already committed to work on the IEP priorities (selected in Part 1). The selected areas should reflect a quantity of learning outcomes that reasonably can be addressed given available instructional time.

d. **Do the areas selected represent the greatest opportunity for and the least restriction on student potential?** Many times the learning capacity of young children is unknown when they start school. When faced with the choice between general education academics and more traditional special education content (e.g., self-care skills, community skills), if the team does not choose the higher level cognitive skills they may be making a decision that could restrict the student as the years pass. It is easier to shift away from a traditional academic curriculum than to return to it later. That is one reason why you should consider the general education curriculum as a potentially viable component of the student's Breadth of Curriculum. The situation may be reversed for older students who are preparing for adult life and need specific community and vocational preparation. Each case must be considered individually with the precaution of not selling students short before we even attempt to teach them.

6. **For each targeted general education curriculum area (i.e., those marked "+"), write the source of curriculum** (e.g., Burlington Curriculum Guide). For the cross-environmental and environment-specific areas, write COACH or any other source of your choosing.

7. **Prepare a list of all the Breadth of Curriculum learning outcomes by curriculum area using the Breadth of Curriculum Listing.** See Figure 13. For each curriculum area targeted for instruction on the Breadth of Curriculum Worksheet (Figure 12), review the corresponding list of learning outcomes and record those that will be targeted for instruction in the Learning Outcomes column.

   When examining general education curriculum areas to be included on the listing, remember that items noted may be from the same grade-level as the student's placement, from another general education grade-level if the MULTI-LEVEL option was identified during fact-finding, or from some combination of various grade-level learning outcomes. If the number of learning outcomes from general education areas is substantial, as one might expect for a student with mild disabilities, you may wish to photocopy the general education curriculum lists of learning outcomes and note on the copy (e.g., by circling or checking) which items are part of the student's Breadth of Curriculum. For examining cross-environmental or environment-specific curriculum areas in COACH, the activity lists (e.g., Communication, Socialization, Community, Vocational) include a column on the far right side to indicate that an activity should be included in the Breadth of Curriculum. Figures 14 and 15, respectively, show how these forms would look for curriculum areas that were assessed in Part 1 and those that were not.

8. Double check the Cross-Prioritization grid (Part 1.5) to make sure that important content has not been inadvertently omitted from the Breadth of Curriculum.

9. **Verify the listings** to ensure that all team members feel they are appropriate and manageable. Space is provided on the Breadth of Curriculum Listing to **put the initials of team members and have them indicate their agreement or disagreement with listed learning outcomes** by marking a "+" or "−." Team members may also add learning outcomes. As mentioned earlier, this **verification may take place at a meeting, over the telephone, or through correspon-**

PART 2.2   BREADTH OF CURRICULUM
LISTING

Student's name ___Tommy Smith_____ Planning for the ___1991-1992___ school year
Do you agree that the following learning outcomes will be *targeted for instruction*? Write a "+" if you
agree. Write a "−" if you disagree. Add other learning outcomes you feel should be targeted for instruction in the blank spaces.

#	Curriculum Area	Learning Outcomes	Initials of Team Members							
			MS/DS	PG	LJ	JK	KD	AR	FB	JB
1	Phys. Ed.	Demonstrates Reach and Pull	+	+	+	+	+	+	+	+
2	"	Uses Gym Scooter	+	+	+	+	+	+	+	+
3	"	Demonstrates Tension Relaxation	+	+	+	+	+	+	+	+
4	Health	Acknowledges Feelings	+	+	+	+	+	+	+	+
5	"	Locates Key Places in School	+	+	+	+	+	+	+	+
6	"	Identifies own Wellness/Illness	+	+	+	+	+	+	+	+
7	Computer	Uses ENTER + CLEAR Keys	+	+	+	+	+	+	+	+
8	"	Locates Letters/#'s on Keyboard	+	+	+	+	+	+	+	+
9	Commun.	Makes Requests	+	+	+	+	+	+	+	+
10	"	Follows Instructions	+	+	+	+	+	+	+	+
11	Social	Accepts Transitions (routine)	+	+	+	+	+	+	+	+
12	Rec./Leis.	Active Leisure with Others	+	+	+	+	+	+	+	+
13	Academics	Reads Symbols	+	+	+	+	+	+	+	+
14	"	Writes Self-ID (rubber stamp)	+	+	+	+	+	+	+	+
15	School	Participation in Small Groups	+	+	+	+	+	+	+	+
16	"	Uses School Facilities	+	+	+	+	+	+	+	+
17	Vocational	School Job with Peers	+	+	+	+	+	+	+	+

Figure 13.   Part 2.2: Breadth of Curriculum Listing.

COMMUNICATION[a]

COACH

PART 1.2

Check only one box:
ASSESS IN PART 1 (Potential Priorities this Year) ☒ ASSESS IN PART 2 (Breadth of Curriculum) ☐ SKIP FOR NOW ☐

			PART 1.3	PART 1.4		PART 2.2
#	ACTIVITIES	SCORE	NEEDS WORK	POTENTIAL PRIORITY	RANK	BREADTH OF CURR.
1	Indicates Continuation or Expresses More (e.g., makes sound or movement when desired interaction stops to indicate he or she would like eating, playing, and so forth to continue).	S	N (Y)	✓	2	
2	Makes Choices when Presented with Options.	P	N (Y)	✓	1	
3	Makes Requests (e.g., for objects, food, inter-actions, activities, assistance).	E	N (Y)			✓
4	Summons Others (e.g., has an acceptable way to call others to him or her).	E	N (Y)	✓	3	
5	Expresses Rejection/Refusal (e.g., indi-cates when he or she wants something to stop or does not want something to begin).	S	(N) Y			
6	Greets Others.	P	N (Y)	✓	4	
7	Follows Instructions (e.g., simple, one-step, or multi-step directions).	E	N (Y)			✓
8	Describes Events, Objects, Interactions, and so forth (e.g., uses vocabulary, nouns, verbs, adjectives).	E	N (Y)			
9	Responds to Questions (e.g., if asked a question he or she will attempt to answer).	E	(N) Y			
10	Asks Questions of Others.	E	(N) Y			
11	Sustains Communication with Others (e.g., takes turns, maintains attention, stays on topic, perseveres).	E	(N) Y			
			N Y			
			N Y			

Comments: *Tommy has no consistent way to communicate that is easily understood by people other than his family.*

Scoring Key: R = Resistant to the assistance of others P = Partial skill (25%–80%) Use scores alone
E = Early/emerging skills (1%–25%) S = Skillful (80%–100%) or in combination.

[a]Communication may be exhibited or received in any combination of ways (e.g., speaking, gestures, signing, keyboards).

Choosing Options and Accommodations for Children • © 1993 by Michael F. Giangreco • Baltimore: Brookes Publishing Co.

Figure 14. Part 2.2: Breadth of Curriculum column for curriculum area assessed in Part 1.

LEISURE/RECREATION

PART 1.2

Check only one box:
ASSESS IN PART 1 (Potential Priorities this Year)☐ ASSESS IN PART 2 (Breadth of Curriculum)☒ SKIP FOR NOW☐

#	ACTIVITIES	SCORE	NEEDS WORK	POTENTIAL PRIORITY	RANK	BREADTH OF CURR.
				PART 1.3	**PART 1.4**	**PART 2.2**
35	Engages in Individual, Passive Leisure Activities (e.g., listens to music, watches television).		N Y			
36	Engages in Individual, Active Leisure Activities (e.g., toy play, games, sports, exercise, hobbies).		N Y			
37	Engages in Passive Leisure Activities with Others (e.g., goes to movies, performances, spectator sports or events with others).		N Y			
38	Engages in Active Leisure with Others (e.g., group games, activities, sports).		N Y			✓
			N Y			
			N Y			
			N Y			
			N Y			

Comments:

Scoring Key:	R = Resistant to the assistance of others	P = Partial skill (25%–80%)	Use scores alone
	E = Early/emerging skills (1%–25%)	S = Skillful (80%–100%)	or in combination.

Choosing Options and Accommodations for Children • © 1993 by Michael F. Giangreco • Baltimore: Brookes Publishing Co.

Figure 15. Part 2.2: Breadth of Curriculum column for curriculum area not assessed in Part 1.

dence. On items about which differences of opinion exist, **provide mechanisms to discuss the differences and make decisions. Cross out learning outcomes that the team has agreed to eliminate** from the Breadth of Curriculum.

Reference team decisions to the student's needs and the criteria mentioned above under Number 5. Do not select curricular content merely because it is valued by your discipline. Any professional wishing to pursue specific learning outcomes should explain her ideas to the team for consideration and approval. **Teams are encouraged to strive for consensus and avoid deference to each discipline;** having professionals pursue their own agendas can lead to disjointed programs and interfere with the team's development of a shared framework and common goals. All team members must have an opportunity to be part of determining the Breadth of Curriculum.

Methods for measuring student progress on Breadth of Curriculum learning outcomes should be considered. Usually, those from the general education curriculum can be evaluated in the same way as for the student's classmates (e.g., skill checklists, portfolio of work, narrative descriptions). Items from COACH or other sources of learning outcomes may warrant use of additional evaluation methods (e.g., program-specific data collection).

PART 2.3 DETERMINING GENERAL SUPPORTS

1. Remind participants that **general supports** are **provided for the student** to allow access to education, encourage learning, or pursue valued life outcomes.
2. Decide what approach the team will use to determine the general supports. Although this step can be accomplished at a large group team meeting, logistical constraints may prevent participation by the entire team at the same time. One option is to have the general supports initiated by the core team, the teacher, or any other *ad hoc* group formed for this purpose. To reach consensus this initial work then can be reviewed with other team members through face-to-face interactions, telephone calls, or by mail. The important task here is for the team to agree on how they wish to ensure team member input within reasonable time and logistical constraints. Team members participating in determining the general supports should **be familiar enough with the student's characteristics, needs, interests, and level of functioning** to offer thoughtful input to the process. The entire team must have an opportunity to be part of determining the general supports.
3. Complete the identifying information at the top of the page (e.g., student name). See Figure 16.
4. In each category (e.g., Personal Needs, Physical Needs, Teaching Others About the Student), write general supports the designated team members believe are **needed** to enable the student to have access to educational opportunities or pursue learning outcomes identified in the IEP goals and in the Breadth of Curriculum. These supports should be quite general in nature, not the kind of specific supports considered at the lesson planning stage. The supports must be educationally relevant and necessary.
5. For each entry, write the number (from Valued Life Outcomes, Part 1.1) indicating which valued life outcome the general support is meant to improve. This ensures that team members understand the underlying purpose for the support (e.g., improving the student's health, making friends, having access to new places).
6. **Verify the listings** to ensure all team members feel they are appropriate and manageable. Space is provided on the General Supports form for **the initials of all team members and indication of their agreement or disagreement with listed general supports** with a " + " or " − ." Team members may also add items. As mentioned earlier, this **verification may take place at a meeting, over the telephone, or through correspondence**. On items about which differences of opinion exist, **provide mechanisms to discuss the differences and make decisions. Cross out supports the team has agreed to eliminate.** Do not select a general support solely because it is valued by your discipline. Any team member who believes a general support is necessary should explain his ideas to the team for consideration and approval. **Teams are en-**

PART 2.3   GENERAL SUPPORTS

COACH

Student's name __Tommy Smith__ Planning for the __1991-1992__ school year
What general supports need to be provided for the student to allow him or her access to learning opportunities or pursuit of learning outcomes? Write a "+" if you agree. Write a "-" if you disagree. Write the numbers of corresponding valued life outcome(s) 1–5. Add other general supports you feel are necessary in the blank spaces.

Category	#	Supports/Accommodations	Valued Life Outcome	Initials of Team Members							
				MS/DS	DG	LJ	JK	KD	AR	FB	TB
Personal Needs	1	Feed Snacks + lunch	5	+	+	+	+	+	+	+	+
	2	Dress as needed (e.g., gym)	2	+	+	+	+	+	+	+	+
	3	Change diapers	5	+	+	+	+	+	+	+	+
Physical Needs	4	Reposition out of wheelchair	2+5	+	+	+	+	+	+	+	+
	5	Move from place to place	2+3	+	+	+	+	+	+	+	+
	6	Passive Range of Motion	5	+	+	+	+	+	+	+	+
Sensory Needs	7	Position close to things	2	+	+	+	+	+	+	+	+
Teaching Others About the Student	8	Teach Staff + peers what his expressions mean (e.g., facial, vocal)	3+4	+	+	+	+	+	+	+	+
Providing Access and Opportunities	9	Bring to all activities available to classmates	2+3	+	+	+	+	+	+	+	+

Figure 16. Part 2.3: General Supports.

couraged to strive for consensus and avoid deference to each discipline. Each professional pursuing her own agenda can lead to disjointed programs and interfere with the team's development of a shared framework and common goals.

PART 2.4   PROGRAM-AT-A-GLANCE

1. After Parts 2.1 (IEP goals), 2.2 (Breadth of Curriculum), and 2.3 (General Supports) are agreed to by team members, a summary of the student's educational program can be prepared; this is called a **Program-at-a-Glance**. Simply list the information from the above parts so it can be viewed on one to two pages. See Figure 17.
2. You may choose to code entries to indicate when they will be addressed during the school year. Use codes that make sense to you. It is important to know if the team plans to work on a particular component throughout the year, just at the beginning, not until second semester, and so forth. Annual goals will be worked on All Year and could be coded (**AY**). Some Breadth of Curriculum learning outcomes might be targeted for instruction First Semester and coded (**FS**); others might not be targeted for instruction until Second Semester and coded (**SS**). This information is important for scheduling.
3. Once all the educational program components have been identified, the team is in a position to make a more specific placement recommendation. Knowing the educational program components is necessary to make an informed placement decision. Placement here refers to the general, age-appropriate placement (e.g., grade 3), not necessarily the specific class or teacher. As discussed in the Introduction to Part 1 of COACH, general education class placements should always be considered first.
4. After the educational program components and placement are known, the team can determine related service needs (e.g., type, frequency, mode of service provision) required for the student to benefit from his educational program and placement. Educationally relevant and necessary related service needs cannot be determined prior to identification of the components of the educational program and the placement.
5. Some teams have found it helpful to attach the Program-at-a-Glance to the IEP as an addendum. Although some of the documentation included in the Program-at-a-Glance is not required on the IEP (e.g., Breadth of Curriculum), such documentation can facilitate the team's development of a shared framework.

PART 2.5   WRITING SHORT-TERM OBJECTIVES

Development of short-term objectives is a refining process whereby generally stated goals are broken down into a sequence of smaller steps. As under "PREPARATION FOR COACH, Part 1" (see page 31), these **Objectives are generated from a single, unified set of discipline-free goals.** Short-term objectives may be written in many different ways. Generally, objectives include three distinct components: 1) conditions, 2) behavior, and 3) criteria.

   Conditions under which the behavior will occur should be included. These are the conditions that are crucial in order for the student to engage in the behavior. These conditions frequently refer to specific **cues** (e.g., "Show me what you want," "Turn on the switch"); special **equipment or materials** (e.g., heavy ruled writing paper, spoon with a built-up handle, time card, plate secured with a suction cup); and/or **contexts**, to include settings and/or times (e.g., in class, on the playground during recess, at work, upon arrival). Conditions may be stated in a variety of combinations. **It is not necessary to include every condition, only those that are crucial and unique in order for the student to pursue the objective.** Also, it is important to remember that, ultimately, it is desirable for students to respond to natural cues in natural contexts (Ford & Mirenda, 1984). Therefore, **assistive (non–naturally occurring) conditions should be used conservatively**, and plans should be made to fade such conditions as soon as possible.

PART 2.4 COACH-GENERATED PROGRAM-AT-A-GLANCE
for Tommy Smith

FAMILY-CENTERED PRIORITIES FOR IEP GOALS (FROM PART 1.5)

COMMUNICATION	1. Indicates "more."
	2. Makes choices when presented with options.
	3. Summons others.
SOCIALIZATION	4. Sustains interactions with peers without disabilities.
SCHOOL	5. Works at task independently.

BREADTH OF CURRICULUM LEARNING OUTCOMES (FROM PART 2.2)

PHYSICAL EDUCATION	6. Demonstrates reach and pull.
	7. Uses gym scooter.[a]
	8. Demonstrates tension/relaxation exercises.
HEALTH	9. Acknowledges feeling.[a]
	10. Locates key places in the classroom and school.
	11. Identifies own wellness and illness.
COMPUTER	12. Uses ENTER and CLEAR keys on the computer.
	13. Locates letters and numbers on the computer keyboard.
COMMUNICATION	14. Makes requests.
	15. Follows instructions.
SOCIALIZATION	16. Accepts transitions between routine activities.
RECREATION/LEISURE	17. Engages in active leisure with peers.
ACADEMICS	18. Reads symbols/photographs.
	19. Writes self-identification information (rubber stamp).
SCHOOL	20. Participates in small groups.
	21. Uses school facilities.
VOCATIONAL	22. Does school job with peers without disabilities.

GENERAL SUPPORTS (FROM PART 2.3)

PERSONAL NEEDS	23. Feed snacks and lunch.
	24. Dress as needed (e.g., gym, recess).
	25. Change diapers.
PHYSICAL NEEDS	26. Reposition out of wheelchair at least once per hour.
	27. Move from place to place.
	28. Provide passive range of motion within daily activities.
SENSORY NEEDS	29. Position close to activities/people so he can see them.
TEACHING OTHERS	30. Teach staff and peers what his facial expressions mean.
PROVIDING ACCESS	31. Take him to the activities available to classmates.

[a]To be addressed later in the school year

Figure 17. Part 2.4: Program-at-a-Glance for Tommy Smith.

A **behavior displayed by the learner** is the central feature of any objective. The behavior must be **observable** and **measurable**. Sometimes people inappropriately write IEP goals and objectives about what they, as teachers or related services personnel, are going to do for the student rather than what the student will be able to do as a result of instruction. Avoid terms like "understand" or "know." Instead write a behavior you can observe that may be an indicator that the student "knows," or "understands" (e.g., points, says, writes, washes, counts, purchases).

The objective should include **criteria**. Selection of the type of criteria is based on how it matches the behavior. For example, if you want a student to increase the number of times he initiates appropriate greetings with other people, you might take a frequency count to determine how many times the student initiates or a percentage to compare the number of initiations with the number of opportunities the student had during a specified time period. Types of criteria may include but not be limited to: frequency, percent, rate, quality, duration, latency, and so forth. It is good practice to include in the objective a second component that indicates how stable the behavior must be before you feel comfortable reporting the objective has been met (e.g., 4 of 5 consecutive school days, over a 2-week period). Sobsey and Ludlow (1984) provide helpful guidelines for setting instructional criteria.

Short-term objectives should assist in the educational process. Like any tool, they can be used or misused. Some people fear that developing quantifiable objectives may trivialize what a student needs to learn or restrict the staff's creativity in planning or implementation. This need not be the case. Objectives can be trivial, boring, and confining, or relevant, interesting, and creative depending on how the team approaches the challenge. Under the best circumstances, objectives can be used as a map of the path to be taken to reach an identified destination (annual goal). As in any travel plan, you might start out on one path, and later change that path to match new information. Since most schools are in session for approximately 40 weeks, it is suggested that three or four objectives be written for each goal, marking intervals of approximately 10–12 weeks. Like most things related to education, objectives are never perfect and often are in a state of change. Therefore, while setting objectives is a valuable activity, it is important not to become bogged down with excessive details or precision since they probably will need readjustment later. The initial set of short-term objectives are your team's "best guess" at the time given current information.

Suggested Steps for Developing Short-Term Objectives

1. If there has been any significant time span between when the annual goal was written and when the objectives are developed, the **goal should be verified to ensure that it is still appropriate**. If not, it should be omitted or modified accordingly. This will happen most frequently when goals are written in the spring and objectives are written that following fall.

2. Briefly **describe the student's current level of performance** related to the stated annual goal. How well does she engage in this behavior now and/or has she engaged in this behavior in the past?

3. **Clarify the intent of the annual goal** by selecting aspects of the behavior your team plans to address. First, consider all the primary component areas that are needs for the student, then select which one(s) will be the focus of the objectives. These components may include but not be limited to:

   - Desensitization/increasing tolerance
   - Acquiring core skills
   - Preparation for the activity
   - Appropriateness of tempo or rate
   - Self-monitoring
   - Termination of the behavior
   - Safety aspects
   - Communicative aspects
   - Indication of choice or preference
   - Generalization across settings
   - Generalization across materials
   - Accepting assistance from others
   - Initiation of the behavior
   - Quality of performance
   - Extending or reducing duration
   - Problem-solving
   - Assisting others engaging in the activity
   - Expansion of repertoire
   - Social behavior aspects and manners
   - Retention over time
   - Generalization across people
   - Generalization across cues

4. Restate the **intent of the goal** as an observable behavior. State the goal in terms of what the student is to do. Students with the same annual goal may have different objectives. For example, a number of students have the same goal, "In home, school, and community settings Donna will improve her ability to eat with utensils." One student may need to learn the core skills of holding the spoon, scooping, and bringing food to her mouth. For another student, skill quality is lacking, while a third uses the utensils well but eats too quickly, and a fourth uses utensils well at home but not in restaurants. In each case the same goal would be followed by a different set of objectives matching the learner's needs.

5. List the **crucial conditions** that must be present for the learner to attain the objective.

6. **Write the behavior and conditions in the format of a short-term objective.** (Do NOT include a criterion at this point). For example, Tommy has an annual goal to "make choices when presented with options in a variety of school settings (e.g., cafeteria, playground, classroom)." Currently he is using a photo communication board to make choices. The team begins formulating the objective by writing, "When asked by a peer to choose between playing one of two playground activities during recess, Tommy will indicate his choice by touching a corresponding photo. . . . "

7. Write a **criterion** by asking, "How far do we expect this student to progress from his current level of performance given 10 weeks of instruction?" For example, currently when given choices Tommy responds by touching a photo approximately 40% of the time. When an adult physically guides him to look at or touch a photograph of a known preferred item, he is not resistant. The team projects that he can touch the item 70% of the time in 10 weeks.

8. Add a **measure of stability** to the criterion (e.g., 4 of 5 days for 2 consecutive weeks).

9. Restate the entire objective by **combining all the elements**. For example, "When asked by a peer to choose between playing one of two playground activities during recess, Tommy will indicate his choice by touching a corresponding photo 70% of the time, 4 of 5 days for 2 consecutive weeks." Based on individual student needs, teaching this type of objective may appropriately account for multiple forms of correct responding and/or be taught in conjunction with an objective to communicate that he does not want to choose any options presented.

10. **Write additional objectives leading toward the annual goal.** In some cases the conditions and behavior will remain fairly constant with changes reflected in the criterion. Or, the behavior and criterion may remain constant while the conditions change (e.g., to become more natural). The behavior itself may change while the conditions and criterion remain fairly constant. This is most likely to occur when the student is learning larger clusters of behaviors at a quick rate. Components of the objective may change in any combination. For some students, the series of objectives may reflect much larger groups of skills that constitute activity clusters or routines. For example, related to purchasing, the series of objectives could address: 1) traveling to the store, 2) choosing items to buy, and 3) paying for merchandise.

Part 3

Addressing the Educational Program Components in Inclusive Settings

Once annual goals, Breadth of Curriculum, general supports, Program-at-a-Glance, and writing short-term objectives have been completed for a student, the next step is to make ongoing plans for implementation. Part 3 of COACH provides a system for translating the student's educational program into actual instruction within general education class activities. This part requires a collaborative team to be maximally effective and is predicated on the assumption that good planning is essential for successful inclusive education. Completing each of the activities in Part 3 is essential; however, teams are encouraged to tailor the activities to complement their own styles and unique needs. Throughout this process, the instructional planning team will be able to fold the student's individualized instruction into general education class instruction in a way that can enhance learning for all.

Part 3 addresses five major components: 1) organizing the instructional planning team, 2) becoming familiar with the student, 3) becoming familiar with the general education program and setting, 4) scheduling for inclusion, and 5) planning and adapting inclusive learning experiences. In Part 3 of COACH the function of the educational team has shifted from IEP development to instructional planning and implementation.

PART 3.1   ORGANIZING THE INSTRUCTIONAL PLANNING TEAM

Team membership may have changed since initial IEP development; however, all team members must become familiar with collaborative teamwork strategies and be committed to working toward the student's IEP goals, Breadth of Curriculum, and general supports as determined using Parts 1 and 2 of COACH. To implement the student's program, tasks in need of completion and the distribution of responsibilities among team members must be determined.

The team decides what regularly occurring activities are to be completed and who is responsible to ensure implementation of teaching strategies. For each activity identified, one team member should be assigned primary responsibility, although other members may assist. This avoids overlap and misunderstandings regarding individual responsibilities and expectations. For example, several team members might participate in gathering, making, and adapting science materials, although the classroom teacher may be primarily responsible for making sure they are prepared and ready for use. Activities for which primary responsibility may be delegated include:

1. Scheduling and information sharing with related service providers and other consultants
2. Being the primary contact person for the parents
3. Ensuring all required paperwork is up to date
4. Training and supervising instructional assistants
5. Channeling information between core and extended team members and checking for consensus on decisions (e.g., use of instructional methods or about upcoming lesson content)
6. Maintaining adaptive or specialized equipment (e.g., programming a communication device, arranging for repairs, locating and overseeing use of tube feeding apparatus, cleaning personal hygiene areas)
7. Gathering, making, or adapting instructional materials

Team meetings are scheduled on a regular basis and decisions must be made regarding organization and communication (e.g., agenda, rotation of roles such as facilitator and recorder, methods of communication between team meetings). These team meetings will provide a forum for completing Part 3 activities and engaging in day-to-day problem-solving. The team can refer to the Self-Monitoring and Peer Coaching Guide to COACH (Appendix C) for reminders about team tasks. The team decides which team members will be expected to attend all team meetings (e.g., core team members) and how extended team members will be involved.

One person on the team should be designated to channel information between core and extended team members. At the elementary school level, music, art, physical education, and library teachers who see the student regularly need pertinent information. In departmentalized programs or high schools there may be several content area teachers who should be involved in decision-making and problem-solving.

Identifying time for planning educational activities and adaptations is critical. Inclusion-oriented schools have developed a variety of options to make time available for planning. Some of these options include team teaching to cover classes; rotating teacher assistants or substitutes; considering special education team meetings as a school duty, along with monitoring recess and the lunchroom so that teachers with challenging students do not have double duty; and arranging the school schedule to allow for common planning periods among team members. Some of these options will require administrative support. Use of basic team meeting guidelines (e.g., establishing the purpose of the meeting, having an agenda, rotating roles, keeping to time parameters, taking time to discuss how the meetings are going) can facilitate efficient use of existing team meeting time. Each team decides how frequently to meet and how long meetings should last and establishes ways to evaluate whether their team meeting time is being used efficiently.

PART 3.2   BECOMING FAMILIAR WITH THE STUDENT

As the team is becoming organized, the second preparatory activity is for all team members to become **familiar with the student**, if they are not already. Team members should have student-specific information regarding goals and objectives, Breadth of Curriculum, and general supports. This information is summarized in the Program-at-a-Glance and must be distributed and understood by all core and extended team members. Additionally, knowledge of the student's learning style, preferences, and the effectiveness of instructional strategies that have been used in the past may also assist team members in contributing to the student's educational program. Team members can gain this knowledge of the student by reviewing pertinent documents, observing or interacting with the student, conferring with the student's family, or conferring with staff members who have worked with the student recently.

PART 3.3   BECOMING FAMILIAR
WITH THE GENERAL EDUCATION PROGRAM AND SETTING

In order to offer sound input regarding including a student with special educational needs in a general education placement, it is imperative that all team members have a working **knowledge of the general education program and setting**. This includes knowledge of the general class master schedule, normally scheduled class activities, physical arrangements of various settings, curricular content, typical routines and organization, frequently used materials, class rules, teacher expectations, major teaching approaches (e.g., cooperative learning, whole language), and any other relevant information. Since some support and related service personnel may be involved in only a portion of the student's program, they need only become knowledgeable about the classes and settings in which their involvement is required. For example, a physical therapist's skills may be required to support a student in a general physical education class. In such a case, the therapist may not need to spend her limited time becoming extensively familiar with other settings where her support is not required; although, at least a general knowledge of the overall school experience is desirable. However, a speech-language pathologist who will be involved in developing communication instruction with other team members should be familiar with all instructional settings since communication skills and instruction will be part of any setting. This would be applicable to any team members whose support extends across settings.

PART 3.4   SCHEDULING FOR INCLUSION

Once the team is organized and the members are familiar with both the student's characteristics and critical features of the general education classroom, more specific and ongoing instructional planning and implementation can occur. The matrix activity described in this part enables the team to develop an instructional schedule that allows the student to learn curricular content identified in COACH (Parts 1 and 2) in inclusive school settings and justifies, if necessary, when instruction in other inclusive settings should occur (e.g., community, vocational placement). The team accomplishes this by aligning the student's Program-at-a-Glance with the general education schedule of classes and activities. The matrix is the divergent phase of schedule development in which numerous possibilities are considered.

During this stage, team members **brainstorm possibilities and defer judgment** in an attempt to discover the range of opportunities available for inclusion. Team members are encouraged to consider the variety of options for inclusion (e.g., same, multi-level, curriculum overlapping). During the convergent phase, an instructional schedule is developed by analysis of all the possibilities identified on the matrix and selecting the general education classes or activities that best match the student's needs.

During transition planning, some elementary school teams have used the matrix activity to assist in selecting potential class placements at the same grade level. At the secondary level, the matrix can help teams select the combination of classes that offer the most promising opportunities for addressing the student's total educational program. Use of the matrix should not be limited to considering existing options only; it should also be a tool both to extend promising options and to create new options. When, on the surface, it appears that options are limited, the team may examine various aspects of the classroom program as potential sources of change (e.g., curriculum, activities, teaching style, student grouping, physical arrangement, use of materials, classroom management). If teams challenge themselves by reflecting on their own practices and constantly take actions to improve the educational program for all students, the possibilities for student inclusion are virtually limitless.

Using the Scheduling Matrix

Like the earlier parts of COACH, the Scheduling Matrix is designed to focus group discussions and be used as a tool to assist teams in developing students' schedules. Users are encouraged to tailor the tool to their individual situations. See Figure 18.

1. In the spaces provided in the left column of the matrix, write abbreviations for the student's IEP goals from Part 1.5; Breadth of Curriculum **areas** from Part 2.2 (e.g., physical education, communication, socialization, computer); and the student's general support **areas** from Part 2.3 (e.g., personal needs, physical needs, sensory needs). The corresponding details regarding each area can be referred to on the Program-at-a-Glance and therefore need not be listed in detail on the matrix.

2. Across the top of the matrix, list normally scheduled general education class activities and the approximate amount of time devoted to the activity when it occurs. At the high school level there are typically more class options available. The team should decide which options they will consider first. For example, if the student is a 10th grader and most 10th graders are taking Biology, Geometry, Asian Studies, English 10, Health, Physical Education, and an elective, this could be your starting point. Given the greater number of options at the high school level, additional classes should be considered if the first selections do not meet the student's needs. By starting with the schedule available to other 10th graders you increase the possibility that the student with special educational needs will continue to benefit from ongoing interactions with peers. This approach will also help avoid the pitfall of placing a disproportionately large number of students with special needs in certain classes (e.g., home economics, food service). Information about the classes and length of time need not match the daily or weekly schedule exactly since some classes may be taught daily while others may be taught on a less regular basis (e.g., art, health, physical education, music). This approach compensates for the various types of schedules used in schools (e.g., daily Monday–Friday, A–B days, A–E days). See Figure 18.

3. Team members consider which IEP goals, Breadth of Curriculum areas, or general supports could possibly be addressed within identified classes or activities, keeping in mind the various types of involvement described in Section II (i.e., same, multi-level, curriculum overlapping, alternative). Starting with the first listed general education class activity and the first IEP goal,

PART 3.4   SCHEDULING MATRIX

Student's name Tommy Smith
Grade 3

General Class Activities

Category	Goal / Item	Arrival 20 min.	Current Events 20 min.	Lang. Arts 60–90 min.	Math 40 min.	Libr'/Comp. 30 min	Lunch 30 min.	Recess 20 min.	Science 45 min.	Social Studies 45 min.	Art 30 min.	Music 30 min.	PE / Health 30 min / 30 min	Depart. 10 min.
IEP Goals	Indicates "more"			1			1	1			1	1	1 / 1	
	Makes choices		2	2	2	2 / 2	2	2	2	2	2	2 / 2		
	Summons others		3	3	3	3 / 3	3	3	3	3	3	3 / 3	3	3
	Sustains Interactions	4					4	4	4	4	4	4	4 / 4	
	Works at-task independently			5	5	5			5				5	
Breadth of Curriculum	Physical Education	6		6		6 / 8		6			8 / 8		6 / 8	
	Health	10				10	10	10			10 / 10	10	10 / 11	10
	Computer	14,15		12,13		12,13		12,13						
	Communication													→
	Socialization						16	16						
	Recreation/Leisure	17					16	17					17	
	Academics			18,19	18,19	18			18,19	18,19	18,19	18,19	17	
	School			20	20	20	21	21	20	20	21	21	20,21	
	Vocational	22		22										
General Supports	Personal Needs	24,25					23,25	24					24	24,25
	Physical Needs	26,27,28	27	26,27	27	26,27	27		26,27,28	26,27	27	27	26,27,28	27,28
	Sensory Needs	29												
	Teaching Others	30 (as needed)											→	
	Providing Access	31											→	

Use activity numbers corresponding to Program-at-a-Glance.

Choosing Options and Accommodations for Children • © 1993 by Michael F. Giangreco • Baltimore: Brookes Publishing Co.

Figure 18.   Part 3.4: Scheduling Matrix for Tommy Smith.

the team asks, "Are there any opportunities to address this goal in this class or activity?" If any team member believes there is a possibility, it is described to the team and the number corresponding to the goal (from the Program-at-a-Glance) is placed in the appropriate box. Then the team repeats the process for the rest of the IEP goals.

4. The Breadth of Curriculum and general supports are considered in the same way. It will be necessary to refer to the Program-at-a-Glance for detailed information. In an atmosphere that defers judgment, team members take turns explaining which of the student's educational program components they believe **can be** addressed during the listed classes/activities. The student's potential involvement is recorded with the number from the Program-at-a-Glance (e.g., 15) in the corresponding boxes. Depending on how the Program-at-a-Glance is prepared, this number may or may not be the same as those corresponding to the same item on earlier forms in COACH (e.g., Breadth of Curriculum listing). Other types of clarification may assist with team decision-making. For example, some matrix users prefer to clarify whether the skill could be practiced or whether opportunities exist for the student to receive instruction.

   It is important to refer to the Program-at-a-Glance throughout the process of filling out the matrix for two reasons. First, under Breadth of Curriculum, the matrix lists only areas; the specific learning outcomes are numbered on the Program-at-a-Glance. Second, not all Breadth of Curriculum learning outcomes are necessarily addressed throughout the school year. Some may not be addressed until later in the school year. For example, a home economics class might not be on the student's schedule until the 2nd semester, or the physical education unit on gymnastics may be scheduled for January. Therefore, entries coded with an "*a*" on the Program-at-a-Glance **need not** be considered for current scheduling; they will be addressed later in the school year.

   There may be IEP goals, Breadth of Curriculum items, or general supports that need to be addressed during **some** of the listed classes or activities, whereas others may need to be addressed in **all** classes or activities. For example, feeding the student a snack and lunch may occur at only two specified times during the day, while positioning the student with a visual impairment close enough to activities so he can see them may need to happen in every situation. Some general supports are not necessarily activity-referenced, such as teaching staff about how the student communicates using facial expressions. While this may be an important support, it does not necessarily fit into the ongoing daily routine and should be addressed early in the school year and then whenever necessary on an ongoing basis.

   NOTE: When coding the potential involvement the student might have in each activity or class, the matrix is used to identify *possibilities*. The notations made on the matrix do not necessarily reflect the final schedule of inclusion for the student.

5. The completed matrix provides an overview of the frequency with which learning outcomes and general supports can or should be addressed within general education class activities. It will also highlight "match-up challenges." Match-up challenges occur when limited opportunities exist, or it seems difficult to address learning outcomes or general supports adequately within the general education class schedule. These match-up challenges show up as an entire row or column of blank spaces on the matrix. Many creative solutions have evolved to meet various match-up challenges without foregoing inclusion in the general education class activity. Some match-up challenges may be addressed through problem-solving efforts, others may be addressed by selection of alternatives (e.g., designating time for community-based instruction). When offered the opportunity, often it is the student's classmates who contribute the most creative ideas (Giangreco, 1993). Match-up challenges may be an indication that the activity is passive and/or teacher-directed, with little opportunity for student participation (e.g., lectures). **The opportunities to meet the needs of diverse groups of students is increased when instruction includes more frequent student activity and participation.** A more activity-oriented approach to teaching and learning is generally considered more motivating to students and interesting for teachers and may help minimize the number of match-up challenges.

6. The culmination of matrixing is the development of a student schedule. See Figure 19. This can be accomplished by consideration of the possibilities noted on the matrix and determination of what combination of inclusive classes and activities best matches the student's individual needs. Developing the schedule should account for criteria such as opportunities for: 1) instruction and practice on relevant learning outcomes; 2) individual, small group, and large group instruction; 3) activities that balance choice and "nonprogrammed" time periods with structure and teacher direction; 4) engaging in activities with a core set of familiar classmates as well as opportunities to meet new classmates; 5) following a schedule that approximates the typical flow of the school day for students without disabilities; and 6) engaging in a variety of curricular activities to ensure that the student's school experience is full and interesting.

7. The information included on a student's schedule will vary depending on the situation. Schedules should include: 1) the class or activity the student is engaged in, and 2) what learning outcomes and/or general supports will be addressed during that class. Schedules may also include: 1) time (e.g., Monday 9:00–9:55); 2) location (e.g., Room 234; Biology Lab); and 3) person(s) responsible (e.g., Ms. Martin, Biology teacher and Mr. Ryu, individual aide). Although some Program-at-a-Glance entries may be targeted for attention during specific class periods, the schedule does not preclude addressing other identified student needs when the opportunity arises. In fact, knowledge of the Program-at-a-Glance should encourage team members to be aware of the student's educational program needs and therefore be in a better position to take advantage of unplanned opportunities to teach.

8. Using the completed matrix, the team begins with the first general education class activity and decides which of the IEP goals, Breadth of Curriculum items, and general supports that were indicated as possibilities should actually be targeted for instruction or practice during the class or activity. On Tommy S.'s matrix (Figure 18) three different IEP goals, six Breadth of Curriculum items, and eight general support items were considered possibilities to address during the class arrival routine. By considering these possibilities and the time available for the activity, the team decides which educational program components should be selected. In this case, they started with 17 possibilities and converged on six (see Figure 19), some of which would be addressed simultaneously (e.g., reach/pull and dressing).

9. The Program-at-a-Glance can be used to keep track of the frequency with which educational program components are to be addressed in the schedule by a check mark being written next to an item each time it is scheduled for a class or activity. It becomes increasingly important to be aware of these frequencies as schedule planning proceeds. For example, one would assume that IEP goals should be addressed frequently; if they are not, the team may need to revise their schedule to reflect goals or other student needs.

10. Some teams prefer to present the student's finalized schedule on a Scheduling Matrix form to show the relationship between general education classes or activities and the individual student's educational program components in a more visual format.

11. It is crucial to maintain confidentiality regarding the student. For example, most 3rd grade students do not wear diapers. The fact that a student with disabilities does wear diapers would be considered confidential information. Some staff would need this information to meet the child's needs; others would not need this information. Therefore, be sure that schedules and other identifying information are maintained in a confidential manner that guards the privacy and dignity of the individual.

12. Although the schedule specifies what should be targeted for attention during each class period, the schedule should not preclude addressing other student needs when the opportunity arises. It should be used to guide, not dictate lesson content. A student's individual schedule should help the team plan for what will generally be taught during each class period but not inhibit the student from participating when the general education class schedule takes an unplanned detour due to incidental opportunities and teacher discretion. Knowledge of the Program-at-a-Glance should encourage team members to be aware of the student's educational program needs and therefore be in a better position to take advantage of unplanned opportunities for learning.

PART 3.4 SCHEDULE
for Tommy Smith

(P = IEP Priority; BC = Breadth of Curriculum; GS = General Supports)

EDUCATIONAL COMPONENTS TO BE ADDRESSED IN EVERY ACTIVITY
(These will not be repeated under each activity.)

(P)	Makes choices when presented with options.
(BC)	Follows instructions.
(GS)	Reposition out of wheelchair at least once per hour.
(GS)	Move from place to place.
(GS)	Position close to activities/people so he can see them.
(GS)	Teach staff and peers what his facial expressions mean.
(GS)	Take him to the activities available to classmates.

GENERAL EDUCATION CLASS/ACTIVITY	STUDENT LEARNING OUTCOMES AND SUPPORTS	
ARRIVAL	(P)	Summons others.
	(BC)	Demonstrates reach and pull.
	(BC)	Engages in leisure with peers.
	(GS)	Dress (assist with outer wear).
	(GS)	Change diaper.
	(GS)	Provide passive range of motion within daily activities.
CURRENT EVENTS	See "Educational Components To Be Addressed in Every Activity"	
LANGUAGE ARTS	(P)	Indicates "more."
	(P)	Works independently at a task.
	(BC)	Reads symbols.
	(BC)	Writes self-identification information (rubber stamp).
	(BC)	Participates in small groups.
	(BC)	Does school job with peers without disabilities.
MATH	(P)	Works independently at a task.
	(BC)	Participates in small groups.
LIBRARY	(P)	Sustains interactions with peers without disabilities.
	(BC)	Demonstrates reach and pull.
	(BC)	Makes requests.
COMPUTER	(P)	Works at task independently.
	(BC)	Demonstrates tension/relaxation exercises.
	(BC)	Uses ENTER and CLEAR keys on the computer.
	(BC)	Locates letters/numbers on the computer keyboard.
LUNCH	(P)	Indicates "more."
	(BC)	Locates key places in the classroom and school.
	(BC)	Accepts transitions between routine activities.

(continued)

Figure 19.   Part 3.4: Schedule for Tommy Smith.

Figure 19. (*continued*)

PART 3.4 SCHEDULE
for Tommy Smith (*continued*)

(P = IEP Priority; BC = Breadth of Curriculum; GS = General Supports)

GENERAL EDUCATION CLASS/ACTIVITY	STUDENT LEARNING OUTCOMES AND SUPPORTS	
	(GS)	Feed lunch.
	(GS)	Change diaper.
RECESS	(P)	Sustains interactions with peers without disabilities.
	(BC)	Engages in active leisure with peers.
	(GS)	Dress to go outside.
SCIENCE	(P)	Summons others.
	(P)	Works at task independently.
	(P)	Participates in small groups.
	(GS)	Provide passive range of motion within daily activities.
SOCIAL STUDIES	(P)	Summons others.
	(P)	Works at task independently.
	(BC)	Makes requests.
MUSIC	(P)	Indicates "more."
	(P)	Summons others.
	(BC)	Demonstrate tension/relaxation exercises.
	(BC)	Locates key places in the classroom and school.
ART	(P)	Works at task independently.
	(BC)	Demonstrates tension/relaxation exercises.
	(BC)	Locates key places in the classroom and school.
	(BC)	Engages in active leisure with peers.
PHYSICAL EDUCATION	(P)	Summons others.
	(P)	Sustains interactions with peers without disabilities.
	(BC)	Demonstrates reach and pull.
	(BC)	Demonstrates tension/relaxation exercises.
	(BC)	Locates key places in the classroom and school.
	(BC)	Accepts transitions between routine activities.
	(BC)	Engages in active leisure with peers.
	(GS)	Dress for physical education class.
HEALTH	(P)	Sustains interactions with peers without disabilities.
	(BC)	Identifies own wellness and illness.
DEPARTURE	(BC)	Locates key places in the classroom and school.
	(GS)	Dress to go home.
	(GS)	Change diaper.
	(GS)	Provide passive range of motion with daily activities.

This information may be presented on a revised scheduling matrix if desired.

Given some of the personal information contained in this schedule (e.g., the student wears diapers), it is crucial to maintain the confidentiality of student information.

PART 3.5   CONSIDERATIONS FOR PLANNING AND ADAPTING LEARNING EXPERIENCES TO ACCOMMODATE DIVERSE GROUPS OF STUDENTS

At this point, the team has decided where the student will be during each activity period of the day and what learning outcomes or general supports will be addressed during each period. The next step is to determine more specifically how instruction will be integrated into general education activities. In planning and adapting lessons, the emphasis of the team is on developing approaches that create opportunities for students to have shared learning experiences while simultaneously meeting their individual needs. These efforts are manifested as students with diverse learning styles and abilities learn together. Important considerations for planning and adapting lessons are:

1. Knowing the individual instructional and noninstructional outcomes targeted for all students within a lesson group
2. Adjusting the instructional arrangement (e.g., small group, large group, cooperative group, independent)
3. Allowing for alternative teaching methods (e.g., demonstration, exploration, lecture, discussion, projects)
4. Preparing and modifying materials used during the lesson
5. Accounting for varied forms of student responding (e.g., verbal, written, tape recorded, signed, gestured, computer-assisted, pointing)
6. Infusing specialized input from related services providers (e.g., occupational therapist, physical therapist, speech-language pathologist) to support attainment of learning outcomes or facilitate participation (See Fox & Williams, 1991b for more information on developing lesson adaptations.)

When considering the instructional adaptations listed above, it becomes evident that general class activities may fall into one of two categories. First, the format or routine for some curricular activities remains **consistent** even though the content may change. For example, in one 2nd grade class the teacher typically sets up math instruction so children have individual folders containing contracts listing the work they are to complete. Children are free to move among different stations, which contain various manipulatives and games, providing there are no more than four children at one station at a time. Upon completing their work contracts, the children meet individually with the teacher to review and evaluate their work and develop a new contract. The teacher moves about the class conducting individual conferences, observing student work, and offering assistance and challenges when appropriate. Children are working and progressing at their own levels. Regardless of the math concepts being worked on or the materials and games available at the stations, the routine during math period typically remains consistent from day to day.

In another instance, 9th grade math class may typically follow a consistent pattern that begins each class session with a brief review and proceeds to defining a mathematical problem or situation. The teacher then arranges the students in small cooperative groups to solve the problem. The routine proceeds with large group sharing and discussion and may conclude with an explanation of the homework assignment. This math routine remains consistent although the content may change as reflected in the problem or situation posed. This routine may take 1 day or several days to complete, depending on the content and complexity of the problem. See Figure 20, columns I and II.

Many noninstructional aspects of the school day may also remain relatively consistent, such as arrival routines, homeroom, study halls, lunch, recess, assembly routines, departure routines, and transitions between classes.

The second category of class format is the **variable** format. For example, during science period the class may hear a lecture 1 day, do a cooperative research activity the next 2 days, followed by an independent lab experiment the day after, and ending with a test on the 5th day wrapping up the unit. The next unit may take 2 weeks to complete, and utilize an entirely different sequence of activities and events. In the case of this science class, the format, content, and location of instruction change from day to day and unit to unit.

Consistent and variable formats present different implications for lesson planning. In the case of a consistent format, initial lesson planning for including the student with special education needs

PART 3.5 SAMPLE LESSON ADAPTATION: CONSISTENT FORMAT
for Salinda Lopez

I. CONSISTENT CLASS ROUTINE	II. SAMPLE CONTENT	III. LEARNING OUTCOMES/ SUPPORTS	IV. TASKS
Review homework. Questions, answers	Review engine size problem.	Maintain socially appropriate behavior.	Ask, answer questions using communication device.
Posing the problem situation	"You are a land owner. You wish to sell your land. Use map, math skills (known or created) to determine realistic asking price." Handouts: 1) map with dimensions and angles, 2) group and individual requirements sheet	Mobility with walker Independent task completion Maintain socially appropriate behavior.	Handout materials using walker with modified carrier.
Form cooperative groups (3–4) to complete project	Groups randomly assigned Assign meeting roles. Decide how to complete task. Completed project must include: 1) cover sheet, 2) action plan, 3) individual responsibilities, 4) map, 5) step-by-step method, 6) asking price, 7) justification and implications, 8) signatures, 9) individual journal entries: what you discovered, how you can use information in other situations. Time limit: 3 days	Time management Social behavior Independent task completion Computer skills	Group role as timekeeper Do individual work within time limits. Follow norms for cooperative group work. Collect materials needed by group. Complete any tasks assigned by group and approved by teacher. Design and print cover sheet for project.
Large group sharing and discussion	Groups present projects—process, price, justification. Teacher leads discussion on math concepts used.	Communication Social Behavior	Report on one portion of project to class (planned and rehearsed with I.A.[a]). Participate in discussion.
Assign homework	Create individual problems and apply same math concepts to complete. Include problem description, math process, solution.	Time management Independent task completion	Complete homework. Hand in on time. Prepared and modified in advance by special educator

[a]I.A. = Instructional assistant.

Figure 20. Part 3.5: Sample lesson adaptation: Consistent format, for Salinda Lopez.

may remain relevant for an extended period of time with regularly scheduled review by the instructional planning team to ensure its continued appropriateness. In the example of the 9th grade math class with a consistent format, team members engaged in problem-solving to devise a lesson plan indicating how Salinda would be included while still working on her individualized learning outcomes. As depicted in Figure 20, column III, Salinda's instructional planning team identified which learning outcomes Salinda could be working on during each phase of the teaching routine. She is expected to work on maintaining appropriate social behaviors throughout the class. During different phases of the class, she is learning to ask and answer questions using her communication device, complete tasks independently, improve computer skills, improve time management, and improve her mobility within a room using her walker. Salinda's tasks in math class (Figure 20, column IV) include: 1) handing out and collecting learning materials (addressing mobility, task completion, and social interaction); 2) assuming a cooperative group role such as timekeeper, observer, or encourager (addressing communication, social interaction, and time management); 3) participating in large group discussions (addressing communication and social interactions); and 4) completing and turning in homework assignments (addressing time management and independent task completion). Questions posed by the teacher would be at the appropriate level of difficulty, and Salinda may have practiced her responses in the small group or as part of her homework. She may receive additional or intensified instruction and support from other team members in the class (e.g., team teaching, providing assistance) or on her behalf behind the scenes (e.g., preparing an individualized homework assignment, maintaining her communication device, adapting her walker to hold materials for her to pass out). Ongoing monitoring of both Salinda's progress and any changes in classroom format can alert the team that changes should be considered.

In the example of a variable format, the learning outcomes or general supports addressed during a particular lesson must be based upon the upcoming lessons and, therefore, may require specialized lesson plans. This requires those personnel responsible for planning inclusive instruction to be aware of upcoming lesson content, materials, and activities with sufficient lead time to prepare and make accommodations as necessary. For example, the science teacher informs the team of the upcoming unit on endangered species. This unit will include large group discussions, lab experiments to explore how air and water pollution affect wildlife, and a cooperative research activity in which students must identify the characteristics of an endangered species, identify what is being done to protect the animals, and list what they can do to help. The teacher identifies these as "challenge lessons" because they will require creative problem-solving and collaborative planning to determine how Jamal can best be included and how materials and equipment can be modified to meet his individual needs. The class will be learning 20 new vocabulary words, some of which are highly specific to the endangered species topic. The team decides which of the words will be most useful for Jamal to learn and practice, considering both science class and daily life. The communication specialist needs time to program this vocabulary into Jamal's electronic communication device and engage in some pre-teaching to enable Jamal to participate in class discussions and the cooperative group activity. The lab experiments will require physical manipulation of objects such as turning on a water faucet, pouring liquids, using microscopes, and handling and transporting materials. It is agreed that the inclusion facilitator and the occupational therapist will move materials to lower shelves for access and devise adaptations to allow Jamal to open and close cabinet drawers using an extended hook, pour liquids, and have an accessible microscope.

Ongoing evaluation of the student's performance and the overall success of the activity should yield useful information for future activities. As the supply of ideas and adaptations increases, the time necessary for planning should be reduced. The need to involve professional staff in the process of making accommodations for inclusion is not always necessary or desirable. The amount of time available for teams to plan ahead for challenge lessons is limited. Additionally, teachers often make on-the-spot changes in their lesson plans to capitalize on student enthusiasm or unplanned opportunities. These may be times when team members can use problem-solving approaches on the spot with the class (Giangreco, 1993) . Students remain a vast and virtually untapped source of creative, inclusive ideas. This provides opportunities to develop the class community, generate solutions to immediate challenges, give students relevant opportunities to practice creative problem-solving skills, and distribute the pressure to make accommodations across a larger group of people.

Once team members become proficient at anticipating upcoming challenge lessons, using creative problem-solving skills, and gaining access to all the available resources (e.g., the student, his classmates, related services providers, consultants, themselves), the amount of time needed in team meetings for planning accommodations, and the frequency of identifying upcoming lessons as "challenge lessons" will diminish.

Evaluation of learning experiences and outcomes should be an ongoing team activity. This evaluation may include reflection on various aspects of the learning experience, such as: 1) what progress the student has made toward achieving her identified objectives, 2) what progress the team has made in facilitating and supporting student learning, and 3) whether the learning experiences resulted in changes in the student's valued life outcomes. Ultimately, the purpose of evaluation is to monitor and adjust learning experiences to enhance students' lives.

Part 3.5 of COACH includes general considerations regarding accommodating diverse learning needs. Persons seeking additional information on instructional planning issues are referred to Ayres, O'Brien, and Rogers (1991); Floyd et al. (1991); Ford et al. (1989); Fox and Williams (1991b); Gaylord-Ross (1989); Gaylord-Ross and Holvoet (1985); Guess and Helmstetter, 1986; Johnson, Johnson, and Holubec (1987); Orelove and Sobsey (1991); Porter and Richler (1991); Rainforth, York, and Macdonald (1992); Stainback and Stainback (1992).

In closing, we wish to remind you that COACH, like any tool, must be used with care and skill to achieve optimal results. Such care and skill on your part will mean that you must constantly be thinking about what you are doing, individualizing to the situation you are dealing with, improving your own skills, and judging your success by the impact your team's decisions have on the lives of students and families. The fact that COACH has been revised so many times is a reflection that our field and our understanding of what constitutes exemplary practice is always changing. We offer you the ideas contained in this book as our current thinking at the time of writing and with the recognition that change is inevitable and desirable. We trust that the ideas and skills you bring to the process of using COACH with families and teams will improve COACH beyond our conceptualization of the process to match the needs in your community for the children you serve.

SECTION IV

REFERENCES

REFERENCES

Aryes, B., O'Brien, L., & Rogers, T. (1991). *Cooperative learning in an integrated first-grade classroom that includes students with diverse learning styles and abilities.* Syracuse: Syracuse University, Division of Special Education and Rehabilitation, Inclusive Education Project.

Berres, M.S., & Knoblock, P. (1987). *Program models for mainstreaming: Integrating students with moderate to severe disabilities.* Rockville, MD: Aspen Publishers.

Bloom, B.S. (1956). *Taxonomy of educational objectives, Handbook I: Cognitive domain.* New York: David McCay Co., Inc.

Bogdan, R., & Taylor, S. (1987). Conclusion: The next wave. In S. Taylor, D. Biklen & J. Knoll (Eds.), *Community integration for people with severe disabilities* (pp. 209–213). New York: Columbia University, Teachers College Press.

Bradley, V.J., & Knoll, J. (in press). Shifting paradigms in services to people with developmental disabilities. In O. Karan & S. Greenspan (Eds.), *The community revolution in disability services.* Andover, MA: Medical Publishers.

Campbell, C., Campbell, S., Collicott, J., Perner, D., & Stone, J. (1988). Individualizing instruction. *Education New Brunswick—Journal Edition, 3,* 17–20.

Collicott, J. (1991). Implementing multi-level instruction: Strategies for classroom teachers. In G. Porter & D. Richler (Eds.), *Changing Canadian schools: Perspectives on disability and inclusion* (pp. 191–218). North York, Ontario: G. Allan Roeher Institute.

Donnellan, A. (1984). The criterion of the least dangerous assumption. *Behavioral Disorders, 9,* 141–150.

Evans, I., & Meyer, L.H. (1987). Moving to educational validity: A reply to Test, Spooner, and Cooke. *Journal of The Association for Persons with Severe Handicaps, 12*(2), 103–106.

Fabian, E.S. (1991). Using quality-of-life indicators in rehabilitation program evaluation. *Rehabilitation Counseling Bulletin, 34*(4), 344–356.

Floyd, P., Morris, K., Saha, N., Marusa, J., Ford, A., Caudle, S., Vogel, K., & Bluman D. (1991). *Math applications groups: A strategy used to accommodate diverse learners in a regular education third-grade class.* Syracuse: Syracuse University, Division of Special Education and Rehabilitation, Inclusive Education Project.

Ford, A., & Mirenda, P. (1984). Community instruction: A natural cues and corrections decision model. *Journal of The Association for Persons with Severe Handicaps, 9*(2), 79–87.

Ford, A., Schnorr, R., Meyer, L., Davern, L., Black, J., & Dempsey, P. (Eds.). (1989). *The Syracuse community-referenced curriculum guide for students with moderate and severe disabiliites.* Baltimore: Paul H. Brookes Publishing Co.

Forest, M. (1984). *Education integration: A collection of reading on the integration of children with mental handicaps into regular school systems.* Downsview, Ontario: G. Allan Roeher Institute.

Forest, M. (1987). *More education integration: A further collection of readings on the integration of children with mental handicaps into regular school systems.* Downsview, Ontario: G. Allan Roeher Institute.

Forest, M., & Lusthaus, E. (1989). Promoting educational equity for all students: Circles and maps. In S. Stainback, W. Stainback, & M. Forest (Eds.), *Educating all students in the mainstream of regular education* (pp. 43–58). Baltimore: Paul H. Brookes Publishing Co.

Fox, T., & Williams, W. (1991a). *Best practice guidelines for meeting the needs of all students in local schools.* Burlington: University of Vermont, Center for Developmental Disabilities.

Fox, T., & Williams W. (1991b). *Developing best practice-based services for all students in their local school: Inclusion of all students through the use of a school planning team and individual student planning teams.* Burlington: University of Vermont, Center for Developmental Disabilities, Statewide System Support Project.

Gartner, A., & Lipsky, D. (1987). Beyond special education: Toward a quality system for all students. *Harvard Educational Review, 57,* 367–395.

Gartner, A., & Lipsky, D.K. (1989). *The yoke of special education: How to break it.* Rochester: National Center on Education and the Economy.

Gaylord-Ross, R. (Ed.). (1989). *Integration strategies for students with handicaps.* Baltimore: Paul H. Brookes Publishing Co.

Gaylord-Ross, R., & Holvoet, J. (1985). *Strategies for educating students with severe handicaps.* Boston, MA: Little, Brown.

Giangreco, M.F. (1986a). Delivery of therapeutic services in special education programs for learners with severe handicaps. *Physical & Occupational Therapy in Pediatrics, 6*(2), 5–15.

Giangreco, M.F. (1986b). Effects of integrated therapy: A pilot study. *Journal of The Association for Persons with Severe Handicaps, 11*(3), 205–208.

Giangreco, M.F. (1989). Making related service decisions for students with severe handicaps in public schools: Roles, criteria, and authority. Syracuse. *Dissertation Abstracts International, 50,* 6A. (University Microfilms No. 89–19,516)

Giangreco, M.F. (1990a). Making related service decisions for students with severe disabilities: Roles, criteria, and authority. *Journal of The Association for Persons with Severe Handicaps, 15*(1), 22–31.

Giangreco, M.F. (1990b). *Vermont interdependent services team approach (VISTA): Training outline, directions, and forms.* Unpublished document, Available from University of Vermont, Center for Developmental Disabilities, 499C Waterman Bldg., Burlington, VT 05405.

Giangreco, M.F. (in press). Effects of a consensus-building process on team decision-making: Preliminary data. *Physical Disabilities: Education and Related Services* (formerly *Division on Physical Handicaps Journal*).

Giangreco, M.F. (1993). Using creative problem solving methods to include students with severe disabilities in general education classroom activities. *Journal of Educational and Psychological Consultation, 4*(2), 113–135.

Giangreco, M.F., Cloninger, C.J., Mueller, P., Yuan, S., & Ashworth, S. (1991). Perspectives of parents whose children have dual sensory impairments. *Journal of The Association for Persons with Severe Handicaps, 16*(1), 14–24.

Giangreco, M.F., Dennis, R., Cloninger, C., Edelman, S., & Schattman, R. (1993). "I've counted Jon": Transformational experiences of teachers educating students with disabilities. *Exceptional Children, 59*(4), 359–372.

Giangreco, M.F., Edelman, S., Cloninger, C., & Dennis, R. (1993). My child has a classmate with severe disabilities: What parents of nondisabled children think about full inclusion. *Developmental Disabilities Bulletin, 21*(1), 77–91.

Giangreco, M.F., Edelman, S., & Dennis, R. (1991). Common professional practices that interfere with the integrated delivery of related services. *Remedial and Special Education, 12*(2), 16–24.

Giangreco, M.F., & Meyer, L.H. (1988). Expanding service delivery options in regular schools and classes for students with disabilities. In J.L. Graden, J.E. Zins, & M.J. Curtis (Eds.), *Alternative educational delivery systems: Enhancing instructional options for all students* (pp. 241–267). Washington, DC: National Association of School Psychologists.

Giangreco, M.F., & Putnam, J. (1991). Supporting the education of students with severe disabilities in regular education environments. In L.H. Meyer, C.A. Peck, & L. Brown (Eds.), *Critical issues in the lives of people with severe disabilities* (pp. 245–270). Baltimore: Paul H. Brookes Publishing Co.

Giangreco, M.F., York, J., & Rainforth, B. (1989). Providing related services to learners with severe handicaps in educational settings: Pursuing the least restrictive option. *Pediatric Physical Therapy, 1*(2), 55–63.

Guess, D., & Helmstetter, E. (1986). Skill cluster instruction and the individualized curriculum sequencing model. In R.H. Horner, L.H. Meyer, & H.D.B. Fredericks (Eds.), *Education of learners with severe handicaps: Exemplary service strategies* (pp. 221–248). Baltimore: Paul H. Brookes Publishing Co.

Hamre-Nietupski, S., Ayres, B., Nietupski, J., Savage, M., Mitchell, B., & Bramman, H. (1989). Enhancing integration of students with severe disabilities through curricular infusion: A general/special educator partnership. *Education and Training in Mental Retardation, 24*(1), 78–87.

Helmstetter, E., Peck, C., & Giangreco, M. (1993). *Outcomes of interactions with peers with moderate or severe disabilities: A statewide survey of high school students.* Manuscript submitted for publication.

Horner, R. (1991). The future of applied behavior analysis for people with severe disabilities: Commentary I. In L.H. Meyer, C.A. Peck, & L. Brown (Eds.), *Critical issues in the lives of people with severe disabilities* (pp. 607–612). Baltimore: Paul H. Brookes Publishing Co.

Hutchinson, D. (1978). The transdisciplinary approach. In J.B. Curry & K.K. Peppe (Eds.), *Mental retardation: Nursing approaches to care* (pp. 65–74). St. Louis: C.V. Mosby.

Individuals with Disabilities Education Act (IDEA) (Education of the Handicapped Act Amendments of 1990). PL 101–476. 20 U.S.C. § 1401–1412.

Johnson, D.W., Johnson, R.T., & Holubec, E.J. (1986). *Circles of learning: Cooperation in the classroom* (rev. ed.). Edina, MN: Interaction Book Co.

Johnson, R.T., Johnson, D.W., & Holubec, E.J. (1987). *Structuring cooperative learning: Lesson plans for teachers.* Edina, MN: Interaction Book Co.

Kennedy, M., Killius, P., & Olson, D. (1987). Living in the community: Speaking for yourself. In S. Taylor, D. Biklen, & J. Knoll (Eds.), *Community integration for people with severe disabilities* (pp. 202–208). New York: Columbia University, Teachers College Press.

Kishi, G. (1988). Long-term effects of different types of contact between peers with and without severe disabilities. Outcomes of integration efforts in Hawaii. *Dissertation Abstracts International, 50*(2), 412A. (University Microfilms No. 8901837)

Laski, F.J. (1991). Achieving integration during the second revolution. In L.H. Meyer, C.A. Peck, & L. Brown (Eds.), *Critical issues in the lives of people with severe disabilities* (pp. 409–421). Baltimore: Paul H. Brookes Publishing Co.

Lipsky, D.K., & Gartner, A. (Eds.). (1989). *Beyond separate education: Quality education for all.* Baltimore: Paul H. Brookes Publishing Co.

Meyer, L.H., & Janney, R. (1989). User-friendly measures of meaningful outcomes: Evaluating behavioral interventions. *Journal of The Association for Persons with Severe Handicaps, 14,* 263–270.

Meyer, L.H., Peck, C., & Brown, L. (Eds.). (1991). *Critical issues in the lives of people with severe disabilities.* Paul H. Brookes Publishing Co.

Orelove, F.P., & Sobsey, D. (1991). *Educating children with multiple disabilities: A transdisciplinary approach* (2nd ed.). Baltimore: Paul H. Brookes Publishing Co.

Osborn, A. (1953). *Applied integration: Principles and procedures of creative thinking.* New York: Charles Scribner's Sons.

Parnes, S.J. (1981). *The magic of your mind.* Buffalo: The Creative Education Foundation in association with Bearly Limited.

Parnes, S.J. (1985). *A facilitating style of leadership.* Buffalo: The Creative Education Foundation Inc., in association with Bearly Limited.

Parnes, S. (1988). *Visionizing: State-of-the-art processes for encouraging innovative excellence.* East Aurora, NY: D.O.K. Publishers.

Peck, C., Carlson, K., & Helmstetter, E. (1992). Parent and teacher perceptions of outcomes for nonhandicapped children enrolled in integrated early childhood programs: A statewide survey. *Journal of Early Intervention, 16*(1), 53–63.

Peck, C., Donaldson, J., & Pezzoli, M. (1991). Some benefits nonhandicapped adolescents perceive for themselves from their social relationships with peers who have severe handicaps. *Journal of The Association for Persons with Severe Handicaps, 15*(4), 211–230.

Porter, G., & Richler, D. (1991). *Changing Canadian schools: Perspectives on disability and inclusion.* North York, Ontario: G. Allan Roeher Institute.

Powell, T.H., & Gallagher, P.A. (1993). *Brothers and sisters—A special part of exceptional families* (2nd ed.). Baltimore: Paul H. Brookes Publishing Co.

Putnam, J., Rynders, J., Johnson, R., & Johnson, D. (1989). Collaborative skill instruction for promoting positive interactions between mentally handicapped and nonhandicapped children. *Exceptional Children, 55*(6), 550–557.

Rainforth, B., & York, J. (1987). Integrating related services in community instruction. *Journal of The Association for Persons with Severe Handicaps, 12*(3), 190–198.

Rainforth, B., York, J., & Macdonald, C. (1992). *Collaborative teams for students with severe disabilities: Integrating therapy and educational services.* Baltimore: Paul H. Brookes Publishing Co.

Salisbury, C. (1991). Mainstreaming during the early childhood years. *Exceptional Children, 58*(2), 146–155.

Schaffner, C.B., & Buswell, B.E. (1991). *Opening doors: Strategies for including all students in regular education.* Colorado Springs, CO: PEAK Parent Center, Inc.

Schalock, R.L. (1990). *Quality of life: Perspectives and issues.* Washington, DC: American Association on Mental Retardation.

Skrtic, T.M. (1991). *Behind special education: A critical analysis of professional culture and school organization.* Denver: Love Publishing.

Sobsey, D., & Ludlow, B. (1984). Guidelines for setting instructional criteria. *Education and Treatment of Children, 7,* 157–165.

Stainback, W., & Stainback, S. (Eds.). (1990). *Support networks for inclusive schooling: Interdependent integrated education.* Baltimore: Paul H. Brookes Publishing Co.

Stainback, S., & Stainback, W. (Eds.). (1992). *Curriculum considerations in inclusive classrooms: Facilitating learning for all students.* Baltimore: Paul H. Brookes Publishing Co.

Stainback, S., Stainback, W., & Forest, M. (Eds.). (1989). *Educating all students in the mainstream of regular education.* Baltimore: Paul H. Brookes Publishing Co.

Strully, J., & Strully, C. (1985). Friendship and our children. *Journal of The Association for Persons with Severe Handicaps, 10,* 224–227.

Taylor, S.J. (1988). Caught in the continuum: A critical analysis of the principles of the least restrictive environment. *Journal of The Association for Persons with Severe Handicaps, 13,* 41–53.

Thousand, J., & Villa, R. (1989). Enhancing success in heterogeneous schools. In S. Stainback & W. Stainback (Eds.), *Educating all students in the mainstream of regular education* (pp. 89–103). Baltimore: Paul H. Brookes Publishing Co.

Thousand, J.S., & Villa, R.A. (1990). Sharing expertise and responsibilities through teaching teams. In W. Stainback & S. Stainback (Eds.), *Support networks for inclusive schooling: Interdependent integrated education* (pp. 151–166). Baltimore: Paul H. Brookes Publishing Co.

Thousand, J.S., & Villa, R.A. (1992). Collaborative teams: A powerful tool in school restructuring. In R.A. Villa, J.S. Thousand, W. Stainback, & S. Stainback (Eds.), *Restructuring for caring and effective education: An administrative guide for creating heterogeneous schools* (pp. 73–108). Baltimore: Paul H. Brookes Publishing Co.

Vandercook, T., York, J., & Forest, M. (1989). The McGill Action Planning System (MAPS): A strategy for building the vision. *Journal of The Association for Persons with Severe Handicaps, 14,* 205–215.

Villa, R.A., Thousand, J.S., Stainback, W., & Stainback, S. (Eds.). (1992). *Restructuring for caring and effective education: An administrative guide for creating heterogeneous schools.* Baltimore: Paul H. Brookes Publishing Co.

Voeltz, L.M., & Evans, I. (1983). Educational validity: Procedures to evaluate outcomes in programs in severely handicapped learners. *Journal of The Association for the Severely Handicapped, 8*(1), 3–15.

Williams, W., Fox, W., Christie, L., Thousand, J., Conn-Powers, M., Carmichael, L., Vogelsburg, R.T., & Hull, M.T. (1986). Community integration in Vermont. *Journal of The Association for Persons with Severe Handicaps, 11*(4), 294–299.

Wolf, M.M. (1978). Social validity: The case for subjective measurement, or how applied behavior analysis is finding its heart. *Journal of Applied Behavior Analysis, 11,* 203–214.

York, J., Giangreco, M.F., Vandercook, T., & Macdonald, C. (1992). Integrating support personnel in the inclusive classroom. In S. Stainback & W. Stainback (Eds.), *Curriculum considerations in inclusive classrooms: Facilitating learning for all students* (pp. 101–116). Baltimore: Paul H. Brookes Publishing Co.

York, J., Rainforth, B., & Giangreco, M.F. (1990). Transdisciplinary teamwork and integrated therapy: Clarifying the misconceptions. *Pediatric Physical Therapy, 2*(2), 73–79.

York, J., & Vandercook, T. (1990). Strategies for achieving an integrated education for middle school students with severe disabilities. *Remedial and Special Education, 11*(5), 6–16.

SECTION V

APPENDICES

Appendix A

Scoring Key and
Valued Life Outcomes

SCORING KEY

R = RESISTANT TO THE ASSISTANCE OF OTHERS

E = EARLY/EMERGING SKILLS (1%–25%)

P = PARTIAL SKILL (25%–80%)

S = SKILLFUL (80%–100%)

VALUED LIFE OUTCOMES

1. HAVING A SAFE, STABLE HOME IN WHICH TO LIVE

2. HAVING ACCESS TO A VARIETY OF PLACES AND ENGAGING IN MEANINGFUL ACTIVITIES

3. HAVING A SOCIAL NETWORK OF PERSONALLY MEANINGFUL RELATIONSHIPS

4. HAVING A LEVEL OF PERSONAL CHOICE AND CONTROL THAT MATCHES ONE'S AGE

5. BEING SAFE AND HEALTHY

Appendix B

Blank COACH Forms

CHOOSING OPTIONS AND ACCOMMODATIONS FOR CHILDREN

COACH

Student's name _____ Date of birth _____

Date of Family Prioritization Interview (COACH, Part 1) _____

Person interviewing the family _____

Educational placement(s) _____

_____

_____

PURPOSE AND DIRECTIONS: In the spaces provided write the names of all team members and their relationship to the student. The "Date reviewed" column is used to indicate the date the results of COACH are shared and reviewed with each team member. It is neither desirable nor necessary for all team members to participate in the completion of COACH (Part 1). Therefore the "Date of Family Prioritization Interview (COACH, Part 1)" will be different from the "Date reviewed" for team members who were not present. This review provides a method for documenting the exchange of important educational information among all team members.

Name of team member	Relationship to student	Date reviewed
_____	_____	_____
_____	_____	_____
_____	_____	_____
_____	_____	_____
_____	_____	_____
_____	_____	_____
_____	_____	_____
_____	_____	_____
_____	_____	_____
_____	_____	_____
_____	_____	_____
_____	_____	_____

PART 1
FAMILY PRIORITIZATION INTERVIEW
INTRODUCTION

The following headings represent categories of information and sample statements to be shared with participants. YOU ARE ENCOURAGED TO INDIVIDUALIZE THE INFORMATION TO FIT EACH FAMILY YOU INTERVIEW. Figures 1, 2, and 3 can be used to illustrate some points.

PURPOSE OF THE FAMILY PRIORITIZATION INTERVIEW

"The purpose of this meeting is to identify the top learning priorities for [student's name] that you [parent] believe would improve [his/her] life. We will also determine which of the selected priorities you feel should be included on the IEP."

"We have asked you [parent] to participate in this meeting because we recognize that you have an important role to play in determining educational priorities for [student's name]."

CONTENT

"The areas we will explore in today's meeting are meant to extend or augment general education curricula. COACH includes a variety of curriculum areas that are designed to improve [student's name] valued life outcomes." See Figure 1.

EXPLAIN WHAT IS GOING TO HAPPEN

TIME

"Today's meeting will take approximately 1 hour" (to complete Parts 1.1–1.5).

RATE

"During that hour, I will be asking you a variety of questions. Since there are so many areas to consider, I want you to be aware that I will be presenting questions rather quickly and will ask for relatively short answers from you."

PARENT OPPORTUNITIES TO DISCUSS PRIORITIES IN DEPTH

"Since some of the questions I ask you will be more important than others, I will ask you to go through each area rather quickly so that we can focus on what you think is important. Once we know what you think is important, then we can plan to spend more time discussing those areas in greater detail <u>after</u> we complete Part 1 or at another time."

OUTCOMES

"By the end of today's meeting you will have selected what you believe are the top priorities for [student's name] to improve [his/her] valued life outcomes. We will discuss and decide which of these priorities should be included on the IEP."

RELATIONSHIP OF PRIORITIES TO THE REST OF THE SCHOOL PROGRAM

"While focusing on [student's name] top educational priorities is important, these priorities represent only one part of the educational program. We realize that [student's name] also needs to have a broad school experience. This will be addressed in Part 2 where we will consider other learning outcomes to be taught (Breadth of Curriculum) and general supports needed to improve [student's name] valued life outcomes." See Figures 2 and 3.

NEXT STEPS

"After today's meeting, we will review your priorities with other team members who were not here today. Once each member is aware of the priorities, we will develop goals, objectives, and the classroom schedule of activities."

PART 1.1   VALUED LIFE OUTCOMES

INFORMATION TO SHARE WITH THE FAMILY: An underlying assumption of COACH is that students' lives should be better as result of being in school. **The purpose of Part 1.1 is to provide a context so the subsequent parts of COACH can be directly related to valued life outcomes.** The following list shows five valued life outcomes that have been identified by families whose children have disabilities:

1.   Having a Safe, Stable Home in Which To Live
2.   Having Access to a Variety of Places and Engaging in Meaningful Activities
3.   Having a Social Network of Personally Meaningful Relationships
4.   Having a Level of Personal Choice and Control that Matches One's Age
5.   Being Safe and Healthy

The following questions obtain information about the student's current and desired future status related to the valued life outcomes. These questions set a context for subsequent parts of COACH, and are not to generate in-depth discussion. After this information is collected, the family is asked to indicate which valued life outcomes they wish to have emphasized in the school program during the coming year. Therefore, spend only 10–15 minutes having the family briefly answer the questions. **Reword the questions** to match the individual situation. A summary of the family's responses is recorded in the spaces provided.

#1: HAVING A SAFE, STABLE HOME IN WHICH TO LIVE

1.   Where does [student's name] live currently (e.g., at home with family, foster home, community residence)?

_____

(NOTE: Since this information may already be known, you can record the answer and restate it to the family: "OK, we know that [student's name] lives with you and his sister"; then move on to question 2.)

2.   If everything goes as you hope, do you anticipate that [student's name] will continue to live where [she/he] is throughout the school years?

_____

If not, what would be a desirable place?

_____

3.   Would you like to talk about what a desirable place would be for [student's name] to live as an adult, or is that too far in the future to discuss at this time?

_____

If yes, where?

_____

4.   Is there any place you would like to avoid having [student's name] live in the future?

_____

(continued)

PART 1.1 VALUED LIFE OUTCOMES
(*continued*)

#2: HAVING ACCESS TO A VARIETY OF PLACES AND ENGAGING IN MEANINGFUL ACTIVITIES

5. Where does [student's name] go, and what kinds of activities does [he/she] do that [he/she] likes or make [him/her] feel good about [himself/herself]? Does [student's name] go where the family goes, following the family routine? _____

_____

_____

_____

6. Would you like to see these places and/or activities change or expand in the near future? If so, how? _____

_____

_____

_____

7. ASK THIS QUESTION ONLY IF THE STUDENT IS 13 YEARS OLD OR OLDER. Have you given any thought to what kinds of activities [student's name] might do or places [he/she] might go as a young adult? For example, in the future how might [student's name] spend [his/her] time that is now spent in school (e.g., competitive work, supported work, volunteering, continuing education?) _____

_____

_____

_____

#3: HAVING A SOCIAL NETWORK OF PERSONALLY MEANINGFUL RELATIONSHIPS

8. Besides [his/her] family, whom does [student's name] have friendships or personal relationships with (e.g., relatives, classmates, friends)? _____

_____

_____

9. Would you like to see these relationships change or expand in the near future, and if so, how?

_____

_____

(*continued*)

PART 1.1   VALUED LIFE OUTCOMES
(*continued*)

#4: HAVING A LEVEL OF PERSONAL CHOICE AND CONTROL THAT MATCHES ONE'S AGE

10. What, if anything, would you like to see change in [student's name] current level of personal choice and control that would enable [him/her] to pursue a more enjoyable life? _____
_____

#5: BEING SAFE AND HEALTHY

11. What, if anything, would you like to see change in [student's name] current health or safety that would enable [him/her] to pursue a more enjoyable life? _____
_____
_____
_____

WHICH OUTCOMES SHOULD BE EMPHASIZED?

Now, ask the family, "Which of the outcomes do you feel should be emphasized during this school year? Although all of the outcomes may be important, please pick a maximum of three." **Put a check in the appropriate space in the right-hand column.**

#1: Having a Safe, Stable Home in Which To Live	**Emphasize this Year?** _____

#2: Having Access to a Variety of Places and Engaging in Meaningful Activities	**Emphasize this Year?** _____

#3: Having a Social Network of Personally Meaningful Relationships	**Emphasize this Year?** _____

#4: Having a Level of Personal Choice and Control that Matches One's Age	**Emphasize this Year?** _____

#5: Being Safe and Healthy	**Emphasize this Year?** _____

COMMUNICATION[a]

PART 1.2

Check only one box:
ASSESS IN PART 1 (Potential Priorities this Year)☐ ASSESS IN PART 2 (Breadth of Curriculum)☐ SKIP FOR NOW☐

#	ACTIVITIES	SCORE	NEEDS WORK	POTENTIAL PRIORITY	RANK	BREADTH OF CURR.
				PART 1.3	**PART 1.4**	**PART 2.2**
1	Indicates Continuation or Expresses More (e.g., makes sound or movement when desired interaction stops to indicate he or she would like eating, playing, and so forth to continue).		N Y			
2	Makes Choices when Presented with Options.		N Y			
3	Makes Requests (e.g., for objects, food, interactions, activities, assistance).		N Y			
4	Summons Others (e.g., has an acceptable way to call others to him or her).		N Y			
5	Expresses Rejection/Refusal (e.g., indicates when he or she wants something to stop or does not want something to begin).		N Y			
6	Greets Others.		N Y			
7	Follows Instructions (e.g., simple, one-step, or multi-step directions).		N Y			
8	Describes Events, Objects, Interactions, and so forth (e.g., uses vocabulary, nouns, verbs, adjectives).		N Y			
9	Responds to Questions (e.g., if asked a question he or she will attempt to answer).		N Y			
10	Asks Questions of Others.		N Y			
11	Sustains Communication with Others (e.g., takes turns, maintains attention, stays on topic, perseveres).		N Y			
			N Y			
			N Y			

Comments:

Scoring Key: R = Resistant to the assistance of others   P = Partial skill (25%–80%)   Use scores alone
               E = Early/emerging skills (1%–25%)   S = Skillful (80%–100%)   or in combination.

[a]Communication may be exhibited or received in any combination of ways (e.g., speaking, gestures, signing, keyboards).

Choosing Options and Accommodations for Children • © 1993 by Michael F. Giangreco • Baltimore: Brookes Publishing Co.

SOCIALIZATION

PART 1.2

Check only one box:
ASSESS IN PART 1 (Potential Priorities this Year)☐ ASSESS IN PART 2 (Breadth of Curriculum)☐ SKIP FOR NOW☐

		PART 1.3		PART 1.4		PART 2.2
#	ACTIVITIES	SCORE	NEEDS WORK	POTENTIAL PRIORITY	RANK	BREADTH OF CURR.
12	Reacts to Objects, Activities, and/or People by Displaying Observable Change in Behavior.		N Y			
13	Initiates Social Interactions.		N Y			
14	Sustains Social Interactions.		N Y			
15	Terminates Social Interactions.		N Y			
16	Distinguishes and Interacts Differently with Familiar People, Acquaintances, and Strangers.		N Y			
17	Maintains Socially Acceptable Behavior when Alone and/or with Others.		N Y			
18	Accepts Assistance from Others.		N Y			
19	Offers Assistance to Others.		N Y			
20	Accepts Transitions Between Routine Activities.		N Y			
21	Accepts Unexpected Changes in Routine.		N Y			
22	Shares with Others.		N Y			
23	Takes Turns.		N Y			
			N Y			
			N Y			
			N Y			

Comments:

Scoring Key:
R = Resistant to the assistance of others
E = Early/emerging skills (1%–25%)
P = Partial skill (25%–80%)
S = Skillful (80%–100%)
Use scores alone or in combination.

Choosing Options and Accommodations for Children • © 1993 by Michael F. Giangreco • Baltimore: Brookes Publishing Co.

PERSONAL MANAGEMENT

PART 1.2

Check only one box:
ASSESS IN PART 1 (Potential Priorities this Year)☐ ASSESS IN PART 2 (Breadth of Curriculum)☐ SKIP FOR NOW☐

			PART 1.3	PART 1.4		PART 2.2
#	ACTIVITIES	SCORE	NEEDS WORK	POTENTIAL PRIORITY	RANK	BREADTH OF CURR.
24	Drinks and Eats by Mouth (e.g., accepts food/drink, lip closure, chews, swallows).		N Y			
25	Feeds Self with Hands/Fingers.		N Y			
26	Eats with Utensils (e.g., spoon, fork, knife)		N Y			
27	Dresses/Undresses.		N Y			
28	Cares for Bowel and Bladder Needs.		N Y			
29	Cares for Hands and Face (e.g., washes, dries, applies lotion, lip balm, blows nose).		N Y			
30	Combs/Brushes Hair.		N Y			
31	Gives Self-Identification Information (e.g., name, address, telephone number)		N Y			
32	Responds to Emergency Alarm (e.g., leaves building when smoke/fire alarm sounds).		N Y			
33	Manages Personal Belongings (e.g., toys, clothes, special equipment).		N Y			
34	Mobile Within and Between Rooms of a Building (e.g., walks, rolls, crawls, moves wheelchair, climbs stairs, uses elevators/escalators).		N Y			
			N Y			
			N Y			
			N Y			
			N Y			

Comments:

Scoring   R = Resistant to the assistance of others   P = Partial skill (25%–80%)   Use scores alone
Key: E = Early/emerging skills (1%–25%)   S = Skillful (80%–100%)   or in combination.

Choosing Options and Accommodations for Children • © 1993 by Michael F. Giangreco • Baltimore: Brookes Publishing Co.

LEISURE/RECREATION

PART 1.2

Check only one box:
ASSESS IN PART 1 (Potential Priorities this Year)☐ ASSESS IN PART 2 (Breadth of Curriculum)☐ SKIP FOR NOW☐

#	ACTIVITIES	PART 1.3		PART 1.4		PART 2.2
		SCORE	NEEDS WORK	POTENTIAL PRIORITY	RANK	BREADTH OF CURR.
35	Engages in Individual, Passive Leisure Activities (e.g., listens to music, watches television).		N Y			
36	Engages in Individual, Active Leisure Activities (e.g., toy play, games, sports, exercise, hobbies).		N Y			
37	Engages in Passive Leisure Activities with Others (e.g., goes to movies, performances, spectator sports or events with others).		N Y			
38	Engages in Active Leisure with Others (e.g., group games, activities, sports).		N Y			
			N Y			
			N Y			
			N Y			
			N Y			

Comments:

Scoring R = Resistant to the assistance of others   P = Partial skill (25%–80%)   Use scores alone
Key: E = Early/emerging skills (1%–25%)   S = Skillful (80%–100%)   or in combination.

Choosing Options and Accommodations for Children • © 1993 by Michael F. Giangreco • Baltimore: Brookes Publishing Co.

APPLIED ACADEMICS[a]

PART 1.2

Check only one box:
ASSESS IN PART 1 (Potential Priorities this Year) ☐ ASSESS IN PART 2 (Breadth of Curriculum) ☐ SKIP FOR NOW ☐

		PART 1.3		PART 1.4		PART 2.2
#	ACTIVITIES	SCORE	NEEDS WORK	POTENTIAL PRIORITY	RANK	BREADTH OF CURR.
39	Reads Individual Symbols or Sequences of Symbols (e.g., letters, words, Braille, Bliss, Picsyms).		N Y			
40	Reads To Get Information and/or Follow Instructions.		N Y			
41	Writes Self-Identification Information (e.g., name, address, telephone number).		N Y			
42	Writes Words, Phrases, Sentences.		N Y			
43	Composes and Writes Notes, Messages, and/or Correspondence.		N Y			
44	Uses Resource Materials (e.g., newspaper, address book, telephone book, dictionary).		N Y			
45	Counts with Correspondence.		N Y			
46	Computes Numbers (e.g., add, subtract, multiply, divide).		N Y			
47	Uses Clock (e.g., face clock, digital, alarm).		N Y			
48	Uses Calendar (e.g., can determine day/date, uses to note special events/ appointments).		N Y			
49	Uses Measurement Tools (e.g., ruler, measuring cups, scale).		N Y			
50	Uses Money (e.g., purchasing, saving, budgeting, checking).		N Y			
51	Uses Telephone (e.g., answers, calls, uses public pay telephone).		N Y			
			N Y			
			N Y			

Comments:

Scoring   R = Resistant to the assistance of others   P = Partial skill (25%–80%)   Use scores alone
Key: E = Early/emerging skills (1%–25%)   S = Skillful (80%–100%)   or in combination.

[a] *"Reading and Writing"* may extend beyond written words to other forms (e.g., braille, keyboarding, computers).

Choosing Options and Accommodations for Children • © 1993 by Michael F. Giangreco • Baltimore: Brookes Publishing Co.

HOME

PART 1.2

Check only one box:
ASSESS IN PART 1 (Potential Priorities this Year)☐ ASSESS IN PART 2 (Breadth of Curriculum)☐ SKIP FOR NOW☐

		PART 1.3		PART 1.4		PART 2.2
#	ACTIVITIES	SCORE	NEEDS WORK	POTENTIAL PRIORITY	RANK	BREADTH OF CURR.
52	Brushes/Flosses Teeth.		N Y			
53	Selects Appropriate Clothing To Wear (e.g., selects items needed for time of day, weather conditions, style matching).		N Y			
54	Cares for Personal Hygiene Needs (e.g., bathes, showers, cares for nails, uses deodorant, shaves).		N Y			
55	Picks Up After Self.		N Y			
56	Prepares Food (e.g., snacks, cold meals, hot meals).		N Y			
57	Does Household Chores (e.g., dusts, sweeps, mops, vacuums, washes/dries dishes, takes out garbage, recycles, makes bed, stores groceries, yardwork).		N Y			
58	Cares for Clothing (e.g., puts laundry in designated place when clean or dirty, folds, washes/dries, irons, mends).		N Y			
			N Y			
			N Y			
			N Y			
			N Y			

Comments:

Scoring   R = Resistant to the assistance of others   P = Partial skill (25%–80%)   Use scores alone
Key: E = Early/emerging skills (1%–25%)   S = Skillful (80%–100%)   or in combination.

Choosing Options and Accommodations for Children • © 1993 by Michael F. Giangreco • Baltimore: Brookes Publishing Co.

SCHOOL

PART 1.2

> Check only one box:
> ASSESS IN PART 1 (Potential Priorities this Year)☐ ASSESS IN PART 2 (Breadth of Curriculum)☐ SKIP FOR NOW☐

		PART 1.3		PART 1.4		PART 2.2
#	**ACTIVITIES**	**SCORE**	**NEEDS WORK**	**POTENTIAL PRIORITY**	**RANK**	**BREADTH OF CURR.**
59	Travels to and from School (e.g., rides bus safely, walks to school).		N Y			
60	Participates in Small Groups (e.g., tolerates situation, takes turn, is actively involved, responds to teacher directions).		N Y			
61	Participates in Large Groups (e.g., tolerates situation, takes turn, is actively involved, responds to teacher directions).		N Y			
62	Works at Task Independently at Nonfrustrational Level (e.g., starts, sustains, completes).		N Y			
63	Manages School-Related Belongings (e.g., backpack, materials, books, hall locker, gym equipment and locker).		N Y			
64	Follows School Rules/Routines (e.g., understands what rules are, raises hand, waits turn, no hitting, follows schedule).		N Y			
65	Uses School Facilities (e.g., playground, cafeteria, library).		N Y			
66	Participates in Extra-Curricular Activities (e.g., clubs, sports, service organizations, drama, music).		N Y			
			N Y			
			N Y			
			N Y			
			N Y			
			N Y			

Comments:

Scoring	R = Resistant to the assistance of others	P = Partial skill (25%–80%)	Use scores alone
Key:	E = Early/emerging skills (1%–25%)	S = Skillful (80%–100%)	or in combination.

Choosing Options and Accommodations for Children • © 1993 by Michael F. Giangreco • Baltimore: Brookes Publishing Co.

COMMUNITY

PART 1.2

Check only one box:
ASSESS IN PART 1 (Potential Priorities this Year)☐ ASSESS IN PART 2 (Breadth of Curriculum)☐ SKIP FOR NOW☐

			PART 1.3	PART 1.4		PART 2.2
#	ACTIVITIES	SCORE	NEEDS WORK	POTENTIAL PRIORITY	RANK	BREADTH OF CURR.
67	Travels Safely in the Community (e.g., crosses intersections, uses crosswalks and sidewalks, acts appropriately with strangers, finds destination).		N Y			
68	Visits Restaurants (e.g., orders food, finds seating, eats meal, pays bill).		N Y			
69	Purchases Merchandise or Services (e.g., food stores, clothing/department stores, specialty stores, post office, hair salon, laundry/dry cleaner; knows purpose of different kinds of stores, finds merchandise or service desired, pays bill).		N Y			
70	Uses Recreational Facilities (e.g., movies, arcades, parks, recreation centers).		N Y			
71	Uses Vending Machines (e.g., to get drinks, food, toys, stamps, newspapers).		N Y			
72	Uses Banking Facilities (e.g., deposits, withdrawals, uses automated teller machines).		N Y			
73	Travels by Public Transportation (e.g., bus, subway, trolley, taxi, ferry).		N Y			
			N Y			
			N Y			
			N Y			

Comments:

Scoring R = Resistant to the assistance of others   P = Partial skill (25%–80%)   Use scores alone
Key: E = Early/emerging skills (1%–25%)   S = Skillful (80%–100%)   or in combination.

Choosing Options and Accommodations for Children • © 1993 by Michael F. Giangreco • Baltimore: Brookes Publishing Co.

VOCATIONAL

PART 1.2

Check only one box:
ASSESS IN PART 1 (Potential Priorities this Year)☐ ASSESS IN PART 2 (Breadth of Curriculum)☐ SKIP FOR NOW☐

			PART 1.3	PART 1.4		PART 2.2
#	ACTIVITIES	SCORE	NEEDS WORK	POTENTIAL PRIORITY	RANK	BREADTH OF CURR.
74	Does Classroom and/or Home Job(s).		N Y			
75	Does Job(s) at School, beyond the Classroom, with Peers without Disabilities (e.g., delivers attendance, messages, lunch money; helps operate bookstore or concession).		N Y			
	FOR SECONDARY STUDENTS: COMMUNITY WORK SITES					
76	Travels to and from Work Site.		N Y			
77	Uses Time Clock or Check-In Procedure.		N Y			
78	Interacts Appropriately with Coworkers, Customers, and Supervisors.		N Y			
79	Follows Work Site Rules for Safety, Conduct, and Appearance.		N Y			
80	Does Work Independently that is at a Nonfrustrational Level.		N Y			
81	Works with Others (e.g., cooperates, does enough work, accepts assistance, gives assistance).		N Y			
82	Follows Schedule of Work Activities.		N Y			
83	Uses Work Site Leisure Facilities (e.g., engages in appropriate breaktime and lunchtime routines).		N Y			
84	Applies for Job (e.g., finds potential jobs, contacts employers, fills out forms, interviews).		N Y			
			N Y			
			N Y			

Comments:

Scoring Key:	R = Resistant to the assistance of others E = Early/emerging skills (1%–25%)	P = Partial skill (25%–80%) S = Skillful (80%–100%)	Use scores alone or in combination.

Choosing Options and Accommodations for Children • © 1993 by Michael F. Giangreco • Baltimore: Brookes Publishing Co.

_____
(Curriculum Area)

COACH

PART 1.2

Check only one box:
ASSESS IN PART 1 (Potential Priorities this Year) ☐ ASSESS IN PART 2 (Breadth of Curriculum) ☐ SKIP FOR NOW ☐

			PART 1.3	PART 1.4		PART 2.2
#	ACTIVITIES	SCORE	NEEDS WORK	POTENTIAL PRIORITY	RANK	BREADTH OF CURR.
			N Y			
			N Y			
			N Y			
			N Y			
			N Y			
			N Y			
			N Y			
			N Y			
			N Y			
			N Y			
			N Y			
			N Y			
			N Y			
			N Y			
			N Y			
			N Y			
			N Y			
			N Y			
			N Y			
			N Y			
			N Y			

Comments:

Scoring R = Resistant to the assistance of others   P = Partial skill (25%–80%)   Use scores alone
Key: E = Early/emerging skills (1%–25%)   S = Skillful (80%–100%)   or in combination.

Choosing Options and Accommodations for Children • © 1993 by Michael F. Giangreco • Baltimore: Brookes Publishing Co.

Transfer a maximum of the top five priorities from each assessed area in their ranked order.

#	Communication	Socialization	Personal Management	Leisure/ Recreation	Applied Academics
1					
2					
3					
4					
5					

(R A N K)

#	Home	School	Community	Vocational	Other ( )
1					
2					
3					
4					
5					

(R A N K)

INFORMATION TO SHARE WITH THE FAMILY: First, the family will be asked to rank a maximum of the top eight overall. **Second,** the interviewer verifies the reason for the selection of the priority and assigns a number corresponding to a valued life outcome. **Third,** the family is asked to verify that their selections accurately reflect their priorities. **Fourth,** the participants negotiate which of the ranked priorities should be restated as annual goals and be "Included in the IEP," which should be considered for inclusion as part of the "Breadth of Curriculum," or which should be primarily a "Home" responsibility. **Fifth,** the interviewer will explain how the results of Part 1 will be used and what comes next.

Rank	OVERALL PRIORITIES	Write # Valued Life Outcomes	Included in the IEP	Breadth of Curriculum	Home
			Check only one box for each priority		
1					
2					
3					
4					
5					
6					
7					
8					

PART 2.1   ANNUAL GOAL WORKSHEET
(Use as needed.)

Goal # _____ (Rank # _____ from Part 1.5)

Behavior _____

Context _____

Team Member Suggestions _____

_____

Final Goal Statement _____

_____

Goal # _____ (Rank # _____ from Part 1.5)

Behavior _____

Context _____

Team Member Suggestions _____

_____

Final Goal Statement _____

_____

Goal # _____ (Rank # _____ from Part 1.5)

Behavior _____

Context _____

Team Member Suggestions _____

_____

Final Goal Statement _____

_____

Goal # _____ (Rank # _____ from Part 1.5)

Behavior _____

Context _____

Team Member Suggestions _____

_____

Final Goal Statement _____

_____

Goal # _____ (Rank # _____ from Part 1.5)

Behavior _____

Context _____

Team Member Suggestions _____

_____

Final Goal Statement _____

_____

PART 2.2 BREADTH OF CURRICULUM WORKSHEET

① Student's name _____ Grade being planning for _____

Approximate number of available instructional hours/periods per day = _____

Curriculum Areas To Consider	④ How many of the **learning outcomes** in each curriculum area are potentially appropriate for student instruction this school year? (Check appropriate boxes.)				⑤ Target To Teach? ("+" or "−") see criteria	⑥ Source of Curriculum for Target Areas (e.g., general education scope and sequences, COACH activity item numbers)
	MOST (80%–100%)	SOME (20%–80%)	FEW (<20%)	MULTI-LEVEL		
② GENERAL EDUCATION CURRICULUM, GRADE _____ ③						
CROSS-ENVIRONMENTAL CURRICULUM Communication[a]						
Socialization[a]						
Personal Management						
Recreation/Leisure						
Applied Academics[a]						
Other						
ENVIRONMENT-SPECIFIC CURRICULUM: Home						
School						
Community						
Vocational[a]						

[a]Likely overlap with some portion of general education curriculum.

（#） = order in which steps of this worksheet are completed.

Choosing Options and Accommodations for Children • © 1993 by Michael F. Giangreco • Baltimore: Brookes Publishing Co.

PART 2.2   BREADTH OF CURRICULUM
LISTING

Student's name _____ **Planning for the** _____ **school year**
Do you agree that the following learning outcomes will be *targeted for instruction*? Write a "+" if you agree. Write a "−" if you disagree. Add other learning outcomes you feel should be targeted for instruction in the blank spaces.

#	Curriculum Area	Learning Outcomes	Initials of Team Members						

Choosing Options and Accommodations for Children • © 1993 by Michael F. Giangreco • Baltimore: Brookes Publishing Co.

PART 2.3   GENERAL SUPPORTS

Student's name _____ Planning for the _____ school year

What general supports need to be provided for the student to allow him or her access to learning opportunities or pursuit of learning outcomes? Write a "+" if you agree. Write a "−" if you disagree. Write the numbers of corresponding valued life outcome(s) 1–5. Add other general supports you feel are necessary in the blank spaces.

Category	#	Supports/Accommodations	Valued Life Outcome	Initials of Team Members					
Personal Needs									
Physical Needs									
Sensory Needs									
Teaching Others About the Student									
Providing Access and Opportunities									

Choosing Options and Accommodations for Children • © 1993 by Michael F. Giangreco • Baltimore: Brookes Publishing Co.

PART 3.4   SCHEDULING MATRIX

Student's name _____

Grade _____

General Class Activities

IEP Goals														
Breadth of Curriculum														
General Supports														

Use activity numbers corresponding to Program-at-a-Glance.

Choosing Options and Accommodations for Children • © 1993 by Michael F. Giangreco • Baltimore: Brookes Publishing Co.

115

Appendix C

Self-Monitoring and Peer Coaching Guide to COACH

Purpose: The purpose of the Self-Monitoring and Peer Coaching Guide is to assist you in learning how to use COACH and increase your proficiency with COACH. Users of COACH are encouraged to: 1) thoroughly **read** the COACH manual, 2) receive **instruction** on the underlying assumptions of COACH and its administration if available, 3) observe **modeling** of COACH by a skilled facilitator, in person or on videotape, 4) **practice** administering COACH, 5) receive **evaluative feedback** on your administration of COACH from team members or other colleagues, 6) **adjust** your administration of COACH accordingly, and 7) **cycle through** the aforementioned steps in an effort to become increasingly skilled at assisting parents and students in identifying family-centered educational priorities and other program components.

Some people who use COACH do not have access to others who can provide skilled instruction regarding COACH or effective modeling of COACH. Two alternatives to this instruction or modeling are to use self-monitoring and/or peer coaching. The following set of questions can be used by you or a colleague to evaluate your use of COACH. If you are using COACH for the first time, simply inform the family that this is your first experience with COACH.

Directions: For each of the following questions note a score using the key:
   0 = was not done
   1 = was done, needs much work
   2 = was done adequately, but could use improvement
   3 = was done well

Self-scoring should occur **after** each part of COACH has been completed. Scoring by a colleague (peer coach) may be completed during the process. If a peer coach is used, comparison of self-scoring and peer coach ratings may provide useful information. It is helpful to use self-monitoring and/or peer coaching for a few administrations and chart your progress. Skilled users of COACH will find that peer coaching can help sharpen skills.

I. WHAT TO DO IN PREPARATION FOR COACH (PART 1)

A. Did the team select a student for whom COACH is appropriate (e.g., age, level of functioning, in need of program development)?
B. Did team members read the manual?
C. Was the potential use of COACH discussed with the student's team and was agreement reached to use it?
D. Is the team entering the COACH process with the willingness to accept and act upon family priorities (e.g., generate a single set of family-centered, discipline-free goals)?
E. Is COACH being used as part of an overall assessment and planning process and is the overall process understood by the entire team?
F. Did the team discuss who should administer COACH?
G. Did the team discuss what other team members (beyond the family and interviewer), if any, should be present during the administration of COACH?
H. Was the family asked if they wished to participate in the COACH process?
I. Was the family asked if they had a preference about who would administer COACH?
J. Was a mutually determined date, time, and place arranged for administering COACH?
K. Were forms copied and ready to use prior to the Family Prioritization Interview (e.g., scoring forms; Figures 1, 2, and 3; and sample Program-at-a-Glance)?
L. Was the cover page of COACH completed before the meeting?

YOUR SCORE _____/36
(12 items × 3 = 36 points as the highest possible score.)

Comments:

II. WHAT TO DO AT THE BEGINNING OF THE FAMILY PRIORITIZATION INTERVIEW (PART 1) BEFORE ANY QUESTIONS ARE ASKED

A.   Did the interviewer share all the information from "Introduction to the Family Prioritization Interview, Part 1" (i.e., purpose, content, time, rate, opportunities to discuss priorities in depth, outcomes, relationship of priorities to the rest of the program, next steps)?

B.   Did the interviewer have Figures 1, 2, and 3 available for use throughout the Family Prioritization Interview?

C.   Did the interviewer position herself close enough to the parents so the parents could see the forms?

D.   Did the interviewer individualize the presentation of information in COACH to match the cultural, personal, and family norms and abilities (e.g., use language at the appropriate vocabulary level and in the parents' primary language)?

E.   Did the interviewer set a tone that was relaxed, open, and accepting?

F.   Did the interviewer check for understanding prior to asking any questions in Part 1.1?

G.   Was this introductory information presented in approximately 5–10 minutes?

YOUR SCORE _____/21
(7 items × 3 = 21 points as the highest possible score.)

Comments:

III. VALUED LIFE OUTCOMES (PART 1.1)

A.   Did the interviewer introduce the purpose and directions for Part 1.1 by reviewing the "Information to Share with the Family" at the top of the Part 1.1 form?

B.   Did the interviewer ask the listed questions as written or individualize them in ways that matched the situation and reflected his style?

C.   Did the interviewer request and record brief responses?

D.   After all the questions had been asked and recorded, did the interviewer have the family select a maximum of three of the five valued life outcomes they felt were most important to emphasize during the coming year?

E.   Was the interviewer sensitive to the sharing of this personal information?

F.   At the end of this section, did the interviewer explain that Part 1 of COACH includes curriculum areas and activities that may enhance the student's valued life outcomes if they are acquired?

G.   Was Part 1.1 completed in approximately 10–15 minutes?

YOUR SCORE _____/21
(7 items × 3 = 21 points as the highest possible score.)

Comments:

IV. SELECTION OF CURRICULUM AREAS TO BE ASSESSED (PART 1.2)

A. Did the interviewer demonstrate that she knew where Part 1.2 was located (at the top of each curricular skill list) and that Part 1.2 should be completed in reference to each curriculum area before completing Part 1.3 on any list?

B. Did the interviewer introduce the purpose and directions for Part 1.2?

C. Did the interviewer present the directions in a way that encouraged the family to consider each area but focus in on a subset of areas to assess in more detail?

D. Did the interviewer present Part 1.2 so participants understood that nonselected areas could still be included in the student's Breadth of Curriculum?

E. Did the interviewer accurately record the family's responses?

F. Did the interviewer explain which valued life outcomes are emphasized by the various curriculum areas?

G. At the end of this section, did the interviewer reiterate that only those curriculum areas marked "ASSESS IN PART 1" would be explored in Part 1, and that others would be considered in Part 2?

H. Was Part 1.2 completed in approximately 5–10 minutes?

YOUR SCORE _____/24
(8 items × 3 = 24 points as the highest possible score.)

Comments:

V. ACTIVITY LISTS (PART 1.3)

A. Did the interviewer demonstrate content familiarity with and knowledge of the activity lists?

B. Did the interviewer complete Part 1.3 with the family only on those curriculum areas marked "ASSESS IN PART 1?"

C. Did the interviewer introduce the purpose and directions for Part 1.3?

D. Did the interviewer explain the scoring and its purpose?

E. Did the interviewer remind the family that this section would be quick paced, and did the interviewer maintain a quick pace?

F. Did the interviewer score items by asking, listening, selecting, verifying, and recording?

G. Did the interviewer ask the respondent if the skill needed work this year?

H. Did the interviewer explain to the family that indicating a skill does not need work may be done because: the student is sufficiently proficient given his age, it is beyond what could be reasonably expected during the coming year, and/or the item may be more appropriately addressed as a general support provided to the student?

I. Were the wording of questions appropriately individualized?

J. Were pertinent comments recorded at the bottom of the appropriate pages?

K. Did the interviewer keep the participants on task?

L. At the end of this section, did the interviewer explain that each assessed area would be reviewed for prioritization after all the activity lists to be assessed were completed?

M. Did the interviewer complete all the appropriate Part 1.3 activity lists **before** beginning any prioritization in Part 1.4?
N. Was Part 1.3 completed in approximately 15–25 minutes?

YOUR SCORE _____/42
(14 items × 3 = 42 points as the highest possible score.)

Comments:

VI. PRIORITIZATION (PART 1.4)

A. Did the interviewer introduce the purpose and directions for Part 1.4 with an emphasis on explaining that this is a focusing point to narrow the number of possibilities?
B. Did the interviewer review potential criteria for prioritization?
C. Did the interviewer give all team members present the opportunity to suggest "Potential Priorities This Year" based on the subset of items within each curriculum area that were marked "Y" for "Yes, Needs Work?"
D. Did the interviewer present the prioritization process in a way that encouraged the participants to converge on a subset of "potential priorities for *this year*?"
E. Did the interviewer have the parents/student do the ranking?
F. Was the selection and ranking of an area (e.g., Communication) completed before participants moved on to the next area?
G. Did the interviewer explain that a maximum of the top five priorities from each assessed area would be examined again in Part 1.5 (Cross-Prioritization)?
H. Was Part 1.4 completed in approximately 13–15 minutes?

YOUR SCORE _____/24
(8 items × 3 = 24 points as the highest possible score.)

Comments:

VII. CROSS-PRIORITIZATION (PART 1.5)

A. Did the interviewer transfer a maximum of the top five priorities from each assessed curriculum area to the Cross-Prioritization grid in ranked order?
B. Did the interviewer introduce the purpose and directions for Part 1.5 and emphasize that selected activities are meant to be priorities for the coming year?
C. Did the interviewer review criteria for prioritization?
D. Did the interviewer have the parents/student do the ranking?
E. Did the interviewer have the parents/student verify their overall rankings?
F. Did the interviewer record a number corresponding to a valued life outcome that matched the family's reason for selecting the priority, and was this verified with the family?

G. Did the interviewer explain and guide the process of negotiating which priorities should be marked: "Included in the IEP;" "Home;" or "Breadth of Curriculum" and *mark only one box* for each ranked priority?

H. Did the interviewer review the outcomes at the end of the session and entertain questions/clarification?

I. At the end of this section, did the interviewer explain the next steps (e.g., review results of Part 1 with team members not in attendance; make plans to complete Part 2)?

J. Was Part 1.5 completed in approximately 13–15 minutes?

YOUR SCORE _____/30
(10 items × 3 = 30 points as the highest possible score.)

Comments:

VIII. FOLLOW UP (PART 1)

A. Did the interviewer make arrangements to provide a copy of Part 1 results to the family?

B. Did the interviewer review the outcomes of Part 1 with all listed team members not present during the Family Prioritization Interview and record the date of that review on the cover page of COACH?

C. Did the interviewer work with the team to determine a time to translate priorities into annual goal statements (Part 2.1)?

D. Did the team determine a time to develop the Breadth of Curriculum (Part 2.2) and general supports (Part 2.3)?

YOUR SCORE _____/12
(4 items × 3 = 12 points as the highest possible score.)

Comments:

SUMMARY OF SCORES FOR PART 1

I.	_____	out of 36 =	_____%
II.	_____	out of 21 =	_____%
III.	_____	out of 21 =	_____%
IV.	_____	out of 24 =	_____%
V.	_____	out of 42 =	_____%
VI.	_____	out of 24 =	_____%
VII.	_____	out of 30 =	_____%
VIII.	_____	out of 12 =	_____%
TOTAL	_____	out of 210 =	_____%

OVERALL COMMENTS:

PLANS FOR IMPROVEMENT:

IX. RESTATING PRIORITIES AS ANNUAL GOALS (PART 2.1)

A. Did the team decide who would initiate writing the annual goal statements based on the priorities marked "Included in the IEP" in Part 1.5?

B. Were annual goals written reflecting the family's priorities and their intentions as identified in the valued life outcomes column in Part 1.5?

C. Did the team write annual goals addressing all family priorities, without adding other goals selected by individual team members (e.g., therapy goals)?

D. Did each annual goal include a learner behavior attainable within 1 year and a context in which the behavior will occur?

E. Once the initial annual goals were drafted, were they reviewed and verified with all appropriate team members?

YOUR SCORE _____/15
(5 items × 3 = 15 points as the highest possible score.)

Comments:

X. BREADTH OF CURRICULUM (PART 2.2)

A. Did the team determine which members would be responsible for initiating Breadth of Curriculum?

B. Did team members become familiar with the content of the general education curriculum?

C. Did team members completing Breadth of Curriculum have the general education curriculum available for a reference?

D. Are the team members familiar enough with the student's characteristics, needs, interests, and level of functioning to offer thoughtful input to the Breadth of Curriculum process?

E. Did the team members completing Breadth of Curriculum fill in the identifying information at the top of the page and indicate the grade level placement being planned for in the appropriate space?

F. Were the general education curriculum areas for the grade placement recorded in the appropriate spaces?

G. Were each of the general education and COACH curriculum areas considered and a box marked to indicate the extent of learning outcomes appropriately addressed for the student (e.g., most, some, few, multi-level)?

H. After considering all the curriculum areas, did the team members completing the Breadth of Curriculum indicate which areas would be targeted for instruction by placing a " + " or " – " in the appropriate boxes?

I. Did the team members specify which learning outcomes would be addressed within targeted curriculum areas?

J. Did the team members summarize this section by preparing "Breadth of Curriculum Listing?"

K. Did the team members verify "Breadth of Curriculum Listing" with the team members who did not participate in the initial development of "Breadth of Curriculum" and make modifications as necessary?

YOUR SCORE _____/33
(11 items × 3 = 33 points as the highest possible score.)

Comments:

XI. GENERAL SUPPORTS (PART 2.3)

A. Do team members have a clear understanding of what general supports are?

B. Has the team determined which members will be responsible for initiating general supports?

C. Are the team members familiar enough with the student's characteristics, needs, interests, and level of functioning to offer thoughtful input to the general supports process?

D. In each general support category (e.g., personal needs, physical needs), have the team members listed things that need to be done for the student?

E. For each listed entry, have team members indicated which valued life outcome(s) are being addressed by the support?

F. Did the team members verify the general supports with the team members who did not participate in the initial development of the general supports and make modifications as necessary?

YOUR SCORE _____/18
(6 items × 3 = 18 points as the highest possible score.)

Comments:

XII. PROGRAM-AT-A-GLANCE (PART 2.4)

A. Did a designated team member summarize Part 2.1 ("IEP Goals"), Part 2.2 ("Breadth of Curriculum"), and Part 2.3 ("General Supports") as the Program-at-a-Glance?

B. Were all entries coded or otherwise noted if they were to be addressed later in the school year?

C. Was the Program-at-a-Glance distributed to all team members?

D. Once the Program-at-a-Glance was completed, did the team arrange a time to make related services decisions based on the student's identified educational program components?

YOUR SCORE _____ /12
(4 items × 3 = 12 points as the highest possible score.)

Comments:

XIII. SHORT-TERM OBJECTIVES (PART 2.5)

A. Prior to developing short-term objectives, did the team reach consensus about which members were required to support various learning outcomes?

B. Did the team arrange for subteams to write objectives based on their agreed upon decisions regarding who needs to support various learning outcomes?

C. Were objectives written as intermediate steps leading toward the attainment of the annual goals?

D. Were the objectives written with conditions, behavior, and criteria?

E. Did the objectives clarify the intent of the annual goals?

F. Were the objectives relatively interesting and expanding rather than boring and confining?

G. Were the objectives reviewed with relevant team members and adjusted accordingly?

YOUR SCORE _____ /21
(7 items × 3 = 21 points as the highest possible score.)

Comments:

SUMMARY OF SCORES FOR PART 2

IX.	_____ out of 15 =	_____ %
X.	_____ out of 33 =	_____ %
XI.	_____ out of 18 =	_____ %
XII.	_____ out of 12 =	_____ %
XIII.	_____ out of 21 =	_____ %
TOTAL	_____ out of 99 =	_____ %

OVERALL COMMENTS:

PLANS FOR IMPROVEMENT:

XIV. ADDRESSING EDUCATIONAL PROGRAM COMPONENTS IN INCLUSIVE SETTINGS (PARTS 3.1–3.4)

A. Did the team reorganize itself to prepare for instructional planning?
B. Did team members become familiar with the student?
C. Did team members become knowledgeable about the general education program and setting?
D. Did the team determine which members would be responsible for initiating the Scheduling Matrix?
E. Was the Scheduling Matrix filled out with general education class activities across the top and educational program components down the side?
F. Did team members defer judgment while identifying the possibilities for addressing the student's educational components in class activities?
G. Did the team identify any match-up challenges and make decisions about them?
H. Did the team use the information from the matrix to develop a student schedule?
I. Did the team take precautions to ensure the confidentiality of student information?
J. Did the team review the finalized schedule and make necessary adjustments?

YOUR SCORE _____/30
(10 items × 3 = 30 points as the highest possible score.)

Comments:

XV. CONSIDERATIONS FOR PLANNING AND ADAPTING LEARNING EXPERIENCES TO ACCOMMODATE DIVERSE GROUPS OF STUDENTS (PART 3.5)

A. Did the team design learning experiences that allow students with diverse learning styles and abilities to learn together?

B. Did team members become aware of the learning outcomes sought for students without disabilities in the class?

C. Did the team explore potential changes in the instructional arrangement (e.g., small group, large group, cooperative group)?

D. Did the team explore the use of alternative teaching methods (e.g., demonstration, exploration, discussion, projects)?

E. Did the team explore modifying material used during the lesson?

F. Did the team explore changing the form of student responding (e.g., verbal, written, taped, gestured, computer-assisted)?

G. Did the team explore infusing the input of related service providers in the lesson?

H. Did the team develop a mechanism for evaluating the student's learning and their teaching?

I. Did the team develop mechanisms and procedures for monitoring and adjusting instruction?

YOUR SCORE _____/27
(9 items $\times$ 3 = 27 points as the highest possible score.)

Comments:

SUMMARY OF SCORES FOR PART 3

XIV. _____ out of 30 = _____%
XV. _____ out of 27 = _____%

TOTAL _____ out of 57 = _____%

OVERALL COMMENTS:

PLANS FOR IMPROVEMENT:

Appendix D

Kindergarten Student with Dual Sensory Impairments (Complete Example)

APPENDIX D: STUDENT DESCRIPTION

Keisha Murphy is 5 years old and lives at home with her father, mother, 10-year-old sister, and 8-year-old brother in an urban neighborhood. Her house is two blocks from the school and about a mile from the nearest city park. Keisha has dual sensory impairments. She is legally blind, with vision acuity of 20/200; she also has a moderate hearing loss. She wears corrective lenses and bilateral hearing aids. Keisha communicates using signs and some speech. She understands some spoken language. Signing must be done within one foot of her face or into her hand. Keisha is able to get around most places once familiar with them. She really likes playing active games; she especially enjoys swimming and playground equipment like swings. She functions in the moderate range of cognitive impairment. Keisha is fond of listening to stories and has recently begun showing an interest in learning letters in large print. At the beginning of the school year Keisha transitioned from an early childhood special education program to the kindergarten in her neighborhood. She walks to school with her brother (who attends the same school) and some neighborhood friends. Keisha's kindergarten teacher receives support from a special educator who serves as an inclusion facilitator, an itinerant vision specialist, an orientation and mobility specialist, and a speech pathologist with a background in hearing impairments. A teacher assistant is assigned to the classroom full time to support the range of students.

CHOOSING OPTIONS AND ACCOMMODATIONS FOR CHILDREN

Student's name _Keisha Murphy_   **Date of birth** _1-12-86_

Date of Family Prioritization Interview (COACH, Part 1) _9-10-91_

Person interviewing the family _Jan Landry_

Educational placement(s) _Kindergarten (Central Ave. School)_

PURPOSE AND DIRECTIONS: In the spaces provided write the names of all team members and their relationship to the student. The "Date reviewed" column is used to indicate the date the results of COACH are shared and reviewed with each team member. It is neither desirable nor necessary for all team members to participate in the completion of COACH (Part 1). Therefore the "Date of Family Prioritization Interview (COACH, Part 1)" will be different from the "Date reviewed" for team members who were not present. This review provides a method for documenting the exchange of important educational information among all team members.

Name of team member	Relationship to student	Date reviewed
Jane Murphy	Mother	9-10-91
Henry Murphy	Father	9-10-91
Willa Blake	Kindergarten Teacher	9-10-91
Jan Landry	Inclusion Facilitator	9-10-91
Kay Lynn Cotrane	Speech-Language Pathologist	9-12-91
Brad Laflin	Itinerant Vision Specialist	9-12-91
Susan Elk	Orientation/Mobility Specialist	9-16-91
Marjorie Beasley	Principal	9-11-91
Roger Able	Teacher Assistant	9-11-91

PART 1
FAMILY PRIORITIZATION INTERVIEW
INTRODUCTION

The following headings represent categories of information and sample statements to be shared with participants. YOU ARE ENCOURAGED TO INDIVIDUALIZE THE INFORMATION TO FIT EACH FAMILY YOU INTERVIEW. Figures 1, 2, and 3 can be used to illustrate some points.

PURPOSE OF THE FAMILY PRIORITIZATION INTERVIEW

"The purpose of this meeting is to identify the top learning priorities for [student's name] that you [parent] believe would improve [his/her] life. We will also determine which of the selected priorities you feel should be included on the IEP."

"We have asked you [parent] to participate in this meeting because we recognize that you have an important role to play in determining educational priorities for [student's name]."

CONTENT

"The areas we will explore in today's meeting are meant to extend or augment general education curricula. COACH includes a variety of curriculum areas that are designed to improve [student's name] valued life outcomes." See Figure 1.

EXPLAIN WHAT IS GOING TO HAPPEN

TIME

"Today's meeting will take approximately 1 hour" (to complete Parts 1.1–1.5).

RATE

"During that hour, I will be asking you a variety of questions. Since there are so many areas to consider, I want you to be aware that I will be presenting questions rather quickly and will ask for relatively short answers from you."

PARENT OPPORTUNITIES TO DISCUSS PRIORITIES IN DEPTH

"Since some of the questions I ask you will be more important than others, I will ask you to go through each area rather quickly so that we can focus on what you think is important. Once we know what you think is important, then we can plan to spend more time discussing those areas in greater detail <u>after</u> we complete Part 1 or at another time."

OUTCOMES

"By the end of today's meeting you will have selected what you believe are the top priorities for [student's name] to improve [his/her] valued life outcomes. We will discuss and decide which of these priorities should be included on the IEP."

RELATIONSHIP OF PRIORITIES TO THE REST OF THE SCHOOL PROGRAM

"While focusing on [student's name] top educational priorities is important, these priorities represent only one part of the educational program. We realize that [student's name] also needs to have a broad school experience. This will be addressed in Part 2 where we will consider other learning outcomes to be taught (Breadth of Curriculum) and general supports needed to improve [student's name] valued life outcomes." See Figures 2 and 3.

NEXT STEPS

"After today's meeting, we will review your priorities with other team members who were not here today. Once each member is aware of the priorities, we will develop goals, objectives, and the classroom schedule of activities."

PART 1.1   VALUED LIFE OUTCOMES

INFORMATION TO SHARE WITH THE FAMILY: An underlying assumption of COACH is that students' lives should be better as result of being in school. **The purpose of Part 1.1 is to provide a context so the subsequent parts of COACH can be directly related to valued life outcomes.** The following list shows five valued life outcomes that have been identified by families whose children have disabilities:

1. Having a Safe, Stable Home in Which To Live
2. Having Access to a Variety of Places and Engaging in Meaningful Activities
3. Having a Social Network of Personally Meaningful Relationships
4. Having a Level of Personal Choice and Control that Matches One's Age
5. Being Safe and Healthy

The following questions obtain information about the student's current and desired future status related to the valued life outcomes. These questions set a context for subsequent parts of COACH, and are not to generate in-depth discussion. After this information is collected, the family is asked to indicate which valued life outcomes they wish to have emphasized in the school program during the coming year. Therefore, spend only 10–15 minutes having the family briefly answer the questions. **Reword the questions** to match the individual situation. A summary of the family's responses is recorded in the spaces provided.

#1: HAVING A SAFE, STABLE HOME IN WHICH TO LIVE

1. Where does [student's name] live currently (e.g., at home with family, foster home, community residence)?

   At home with parents, brother, sister

   (NOTE: Since this information may already be known, you can record the answer and restate it to the family: "OK, we know that [student's name] lives with you and his sister"; then move on to question 2.)

2. If everything goes as you hope, do you anticipate that [student's name] will continue to live where [she/he] is throughout the school years?

   yes

   If not, what would be a desirable place?

3. Would you like to talk about what a desirable place would be for [student's name] to live as an adult, or is that too far in the future to discuss at this time?

   It's a long way off

   If yes, where?

4. Is there any place you would like to avoid having [student's name] live in the future?

   Not with sister or brother unless it's OK with them; Not in any kind of institution

(continued)

PART 1.1 VALUED LIFE OUTCOMES
(*continued*)

#2: HAVING ACCESS TO A VARIETY OF PLACES AND ENGAGING IN MEANINGFUL ACTIVITIES

5. Where does [student's name] go, and what kinds of activities does [he/she] do that [he/she] likes or make [him/her] feel good about [himself/herself]? Does [student's name] go where the family goes, following the family routine? _Goes most places the family does_ _except if it's a place she can't move around or make_ _some noise. Likes to swim, go to the park, go to the_ _store, go out for ice cream._

6. Would you like to see these places and/or activities change or expand in the near future? If so, how? _____ _YES! Go to more recreation places and have more_ _of a variety of recreation activities; some hobbies,_ _sports, etc._

7. ASK THIS QUESTION ONLY IF THE STUDENT IS 13 YEARS OLD OR OLDER. Have you given any thought to what kinds of activities [student's name] might do or places [he/she] might go as a young adult? For example, in the future how might [student's name] spend [his/her] time that is now spent in school (e.g., competitive work, supported work, volunteering, continuing education?) _____ _NA_

#3: HAVING A SOCIAL NETWORK OF PERSONALLY MEANINGFUL RELATIONSHIPS

8. Besides [his/her] family, whom does [student's name] have friendships or personal relationships with (e.g., relatives, classmates, friends)? _Gets along OK with most_ _kids she meets; boy next door; cousins, but they_ _are older, has a "Big Sister"; visits a deaf couple once_ _in a while._

9. Would you like to see these relationships change or expand in the near future, and if so, how? _Yes, a little, although she's pretty busy, maybe more_ _friends outside of school_

(*continued*)

PART 1.1 VALUED LIFE OUTCOMES
(continued)

#4: HAVING A LEVEL OF PERSONAL CHOICE AND CONTROL THAT MATCHES ONE'S AGE

10. What, if anything, would you like to see change in [student's name] current level of personal choice and control that would enable [him/her] to pursue a more enjoyable life? *More mobility, maybe getting ready for a guide dog; easier way to let others talk to her*

#5: BEING SAFE AND HEALTHY

11. What, if anything, would you like to see change in [student's name] current health or safety that would enable [him/her] to pursue a more enjoyable life? *Pretty healthy—needs more activity/exercise; cautious, almost to the point of fear of new places*

WHICH OUTCOMES SHOULD BE EMPHASIZED?

Now, ask the family, "Which of the outcomes do you feel should be emphasized during this school year? Although all of the outcomes may be important, please pick a maximum of three." **Put a check in the appropriate space in the right-hand column.**

#1: Having a Safe, Stable Home in Which To Live	Emphasize this Year? _____

#2: Having Access to a Variety of Places and Engaging in Meaningful Activities	Emphasize this Year? _✓_

#3: Having a Social Network of Personally Meaningful Relationships	Emphasize this Year? _____

#4: Having a Level of Personal Choice and Control that Matches One's Age	Emphasize this Year? _✓_

#5: Being Safe and Healthy	Emphasize this Year? _____

COMMUNICATION[a]

COACH

PART 1.2

Check only one box:
ASSESS IN PART 1 (Potential Priorities this Year) ☒ ASSESS IN PART 2 (Breadth of Curriculum) ☐ SKIP FOR NOW ☐

#	ACTIVITIES	SCORE	PART 1.3 NEEDS WORK	PART 1.4 POTENTIAL PRIORITY	RANK	PART 2.2 BREADTH OF CURR.
1	Indicates Continuation or Expresses More (e.g., makes sound or movement when desired interaction stops to indicate he or she would like eating, playing, and so forth to continue).	S	Ⓝ Y			
2	Makes Choices when Presented with Options.	S	Ⓝ Y			
3	Makes Requests (e.g., for objects, food, interactions, activities, assistance).	S	Ⓝ Y			
4	Summons Others (e.g., has an acceptable way to call others to him or her).	S	Ⓝ Y			
5	Expresses Rejection/Refusal (e.g., indicates when he or she wants something to stop or does not want something to begin).	S	Ⓝ Y			
6	Greets Others.	P	N Ⓨ	✓	4	
7	Follows Instructions (e.g., simple, one-step, or multi-step directions).	P	Ⓝ Y			
8	Describes Events, Objects, Interactions, and so forth (e.g., uses vocabulary, nouns, verbs, adjectives).	P	N Ⓨ	✓	1	
9	Responds to Questions (e.g., if asked a question he or she will attempt to answer).	P	N Ⓨ			
10	Asks Questions of Others.	P	N Ⓨ	✓	2	
11	Sustains Communication with Others (e.g., takes turns, maintains attention, stays on topic, perseveres).	P	N Ⓨ	✓	3	
			N Y			
			N Y			

Comments: *Uses gestures, signing in hand, some speech; others need to know how to speak with her.*

Scoring   R = Resistant to the assistance of others   P = Partial skill (25%–80%)   Use scores alone
Key: E = Early/emerging skills (1%–25%)   S = Skillful (80%–100%)   or in combination.

[a]Communication may be exhibited or received in any combination of ways (e.g., speaking, gestures, signing, keyboards).

Choosing Options and Accommodations for Children • © 1993 by Michael F. Giangreco • Baltimore: Brookes Publishing Co.

SOCIALIZATION

PART 1.2

Check only one box:
ASSESS IN PART 1 (Potential Priorities this Year) ☒ ASSESS IN PART 2 (Breadth of Curriculum) ☐ SKIP FOR NOW ☐

		SCORE	PART 1.3 NEEDS WORK	PART 1.4 POTENTIAL PRIORITY	RANK	PART 2.2 BREADTH OF CURR.
#	ACTIVITIES					
12	Reacts to Objects, Activities, and/or People by Displaying Observable Change in Behavior.	S	Ⓝ Y			
13	Initiates Social Interactions.	P	Ⓝ Y			
14	Sustains Social Interactions.	S	Ⓝ Y			
15	Terminates Social Interactions.	P	Ⓝ Y			
16	Distinguishes and Interacts Differently with Familiar People, Acquaintances, and Strangers.	S	Ⓝ Y			
17	Maintains Socially Acceptable Behavior when Alone and/or with Others.	S	N Ⓨ	✓	3	
18	Accepts Assistance from Others.	S	Ⓝ Y			
19	Offers Assistance to Others.	P	N Ⓨ	✓	4	
20	Accepts Transitions Between Routine Activities.	S	Ⓝ Y			
21	Accepts Unexpected Changes in Routine.	P	N Ⓨ			
22	Shares with Others.	P	N Ⓨ	✓	1	
23	Takes Turns.	P	N Ⓨ	✓	2	
			N Y			
			N Y			
			N Y			

Comments: Understands the concept of sharing, but sometimes gets into disagreements with peers over toys; this happens when a child approaches and asks to share but Keisha does not receive the message; when the child stops asking and tries to take the toy, Keisha's response can be aggressive. Need to teach the kids how to talk to her and work on her response.

Scoring   R = Resistant to the assistance of others   P = Partial skill (25%–80%)   Use scores alone
Key: E = Early/emerging skills (1%–25%)   S = Skillful (80%–100%)   or in combination.

Choosing Options and Accommodations for Children • © 1993 by Michael F. Giangreco • Baltimore: Brookes Publishing Co.

PERSONAL MANAGEMENT

PART 1.2

Check only one box:
ASSESS IN PART 1 (Potential Priorities this Year) ☒ ASSESS IN PART 2 (Breadth of Curriculum) ☐ SKIP FOR NOW ☐

		PART 1.3		PART 1.4		PART 2.2
#	ACTIVITIES	SCORE	NEEDS WORK	POTENTIAL PRIORITY	RANK	BREADTH OF CURR.
24	Drinks and Eats by Mouth (e.g., accepts food/drink, lip closure, chews, swallows).	S	Ⓝ Y			
25	Feeds Self with Hands/Fingers.	S	Ⓝ Y			
26	Eats with Utensils (e.g., spoon, fork, knife)	S	N Ⓨ	✓	3	
27	Dresses/Undresses.	S	N Ⓨ			
28	Cares for Bowel and Bladder Needs.	S	Ⓝ Y			
29	Cares for Hands and Face (e.g., washes, dries, applies lotion, lip balm, blows nose).	S	Ⓝ Y			
30	Combs/Brushes Hair.	S	Ⓝ Y			
31	Gives Self-Identification Information (e.g., name, address, telephone number)	S	Ⓝ Y			
32	Responds to Emergency Alarm (e.g., leaves building when smoke/fire alarm sounds).	P	N Ⓨ	✓	4	
33	Manages Personal Belongings (e.g., toys, clothes, special equipment).	P	N Ⓨ	✓	2	
34	Mobile Within and Between Rooms of a Building (e.g., walks, rolls, crawls, moves wheelchair, climbs stairs, uses elevators/ escalators).	P	N Ⓨ	✓	1	
			N Y			
			N Y			
			N Y			
			N Y			

Comments:
㉕ Can use utensils, but a bit messy. ㉗ still puts some clothes on inside-out and doesn't pick clothes appropriate for the weather; ㉝ Needs to learn to care for hearing aids and glasses; ㉞ O+M needs to continue.

Scoring   R = Resistant to the assistance of others   P = Partial skill (25%–80%)   Use scores alone
Key: E = Early/emerging skills (1%–25%)   S = Skillful (80%–100%)   or in combination.

LEISURE/RECREATION

PART 1.2

Check only one box:
ASSESS IN PART 1 (Potential Priorities this Year) ☐ ASSESS IN PART 2 (Breadth of Curriculum) ☒ SKIP FOR NOW ☐

			PART 1.3		PART 1.4		PART 2.2
#	ACTIVITIES	SCORE	NEEDS WORK	POTENTIAL PRIORITY	RANK		BREADTH OF CURR.
35	Engages in Individual, Passive Leisure Activities (e.g., listens to music, watches television).		N Y				
36	Engages in Individual, Active Leisure Activities (e.g., toy play, games, sports, exercise, hobbies).		N Y				
37	Engages in Passive Leisure Activities with Others (e.g., goes to movies, performances, spectator sports or events with others).		N Y				
38	Engages in Active Leisure with Others (e.g., group games, activities, sports).		N Y				✓
			N Y				
			N Y				
			N Y				
			N Y				

Comments:

Scoring   R = Resistant to the assistance of others   P = Partial skill (25%–80%)   Use scores alone
Key: E = Early/emerging skills (1%–25%)   S = Skillful (80%–100%)   or in combination.

Choosing Options and Accommodations for Children • © 1993 by Michael F. Giangreco • Baltimore: Brookes Publishing Co.

APPLIED ACADEMICS^a

PART 1.2

Check only one box:
ASSESS IN PART 1 (Potential Priorities this Year) ☒ ASSESS IN PART 2 (Breadth of Curriculum) ☐ SKIP FOR NOW ☐

#	ACTIVITIES	SCORE	NEEDS WORK	POTENTIAL PRIORITY	RANK	BREADTH OF CURR.
				PART 1.3	PART 1.4	PART 2.2
39	Reads Individual Symbols or Sequences of Symbols (e.g., letters, words, Braille, Bliss, Picsyms).	E	N Ⓨ	✓	1	
40	Reads To Get Information and/or Follow Instructions.	E	N Ⓨ			
41	Writes Self-Identification Information (e.g., name, address, telephone number).	E	N Ⓨ	✓	1	
42	Writes Words, Phrases, Sentences.	E	Ⓝ Y			
43	Composes and Writes Notes, Messages, and/or Correspondence.	NA	N Y			
44	Uses Resource Materials (e.g., newspaper, address book, telephone book, dictionary).	NA	N Y			
45	Counts with Correspondence.	E	N Ⓨ	✓	2	
46	Computes Numbers (e.g., add, subtract, multiply, divide).	E	N Ⓨ			
47	Uses Clock (e.g., face clock, digital, alarm).	E	N Ⓨ			
48	Uses Calendar (e.g., can determine day/date, uses to note special events/appointments).	E	N Ⓨ			
49	Uses Measurement Tools (e.g., ruler, measuring cups, scale).	E	Ⓝ Y			
50	Uses Money (e.g., purchasing, saving, budgeting, checking).	E	Ⓝ Y			
51	Uses Telephone (e.g., answers, calls, uses public pay telephone).	E	Ⓝ Y			
			N Y			
			N Y			

Comments: *Needs large print materials; may need TDD in near future for phone use.*

Scoring Key: R = Resistant to the assistance of others   P = Partial skill (25%–80%)   Use scores alone
E = Early/emerging skills (1%–25%)   S = Skillful (80%–100%)   or in combination.

^a *"Reading and Writing"* may extend beyond written words to other forms (e.g., braille, keyboarding, computers)

Choosing Options and Accommodations for Children • © 1993 by Michael F. Giangreco • Baltimore: Brookes Publishing Co.

HOME

PART 1.2

Check only one box:
ASSESS IN PART 1 (Potential Priorities this Year)☐ ASSESS IN PART 2 (Breadth of Curriculum)☐ SKIP FOR NOW ☒

		PART 1.3		PART 1.4		PART 2.2
#	ACTIVITIES	SCORE	NEEDS WORK	POTENTIAL PRIORITY	RANK	BREADTH OF CURR.
52	Brushes/Flosses Teeth.		N Y			
53	Selects Appropriate Clothing To Wear (e.g., selects items needed for time of day, weather conditions, style matching).		N Y			
54	Cares for Personal Hygiene Needs (e.g., bathes, showers, cares for nails, uses deodorant, shaves).		N Y			
55	Picks Up After Self.		N Y			
56	Prepares Food (e.g., snacks, cold meals, hot meals).		N Y			
57	Does Household Chores (e.g., dusts, sweeps, mops, vacuums, washes/dries dishes, takes out garbage, recycles, makes bed, stores groceries, yardwork).		N Y			
58	Cares for Clothing (e.g., puts laundry in designated place when clean or dirty, folds, washes/dries, irons, mends).		N Y			
			N Y			
			N Y			
			N Y			
			N Y			

Comments:

Scoring	R = Resistant to the assistance of others	P = Partial skill (25%–80%)	Use scores alone
Key:	E = Early/emerging skills (1%–25%)	S = Skillful (80%–100%)	or in combination.

SCHOOL

PART 1.2

> Check only one box:
> ASSESS IN PART 1 (Potential Priorities this Year)☐ ASSESS IN PART 2 (Breadth of Curriculum)☒ SKIP FOR NOW☐

#	ACTIVITIES	SCORE	**PART 1.3** NEEDS WORK	**PART 1.4** POTENTIAL PRIORITY	RANK	**PART 2.2** BREADTH OF CURR.
59	Travels to and from School (e.g., rides bus safely, walks to school).		N Y			
60	Participates in Small Groups (e.g., tolerates situation, takes turn, is actively involved, responds to teacher directions).		N Y			
61	Participates in Large Groups (e.g., tolerates situation, takes turn, is actively involved, responds to teacher directions).		N Y			
62	Works at Task Independently at Nonfrustrational Level (e.g., starts, sustains, completes).		N Y			
63	Manages School-Related Belongings (e.g., backpack, materials, books, hall locker, gym equipment and locker).		N Y			
64	Follows School Rules/Routines (e.g., understands what rules are, raises hand, waits turn, no hitting, follows schedule).		N Y			
65	Uses School Facilities (e.g., playground, cafeteria, library).		N Y			
66	Participates in Extra-Curricular Activities (e.g., clubs, sports, service organizations, drama, music).		N Y			
			N Y			
			N Y			
			N Y			
			N Y			
			N Y			

Comments:

Scoring R = Resistant to the assistance of others   P = Partial skill (25%–80%)   Use scores alone
Key: E = Early/emerging skills (1%–25%)   S = Skillful (80%–100%)   or in combination.

Choosing Options and Accommodations for Children • © 1993 by Michael F. Giangreco • Baltimore: Brookes Publishing Co.

COMMUNITY

PART 1.2

Check only one box:
ASSESS IN PART 1 (Potential Priorities this Year) ☐ ASSESS IN PART 2 (Breadth of Curriculum) ☐ SKIP FOR NOW ☒

#	ACTIVITIES	PART 1.3 SCORE	NEEDS WORK	PART 1.4 POTENTIAL PRIORITY	RANK	PART 2.2 BREADTH OF CURR.
67	Travels Safely in the Community (e.g., crosses intersections, uses crosswalks and sidewalks, acts appropriately with strangers, finds destination).		N Y			
68	Visits Restaurants (e.g., orders food, finds seating, eats meal, pays bill).		N Y			
69	Purchases Merchandise or Services (e.g., food stores, clothing/department stores, specialty stores, post office, hair salon, laundry/dry cleaner; knows purpose of different kinds of stores, finds merchandise or service desired, pays bill).		N Y			
70	Uses Recreational Facilities (e.g., movies, arcades, parks, recreation centers).		N Y			
71	Uses Vending Machines (e.g., to get drinks, food, toys, stamps, newspapers).		N Y			
72	Uses Banking Facilities (e.g., deposits, withdrawals, uses automated teller machines).		N Y			
73	Travels by Public Transportation (e.g., bus, subway, trolley, taxi, ferry).		N Y			
			N Y			
			N Y			
			N Y			

Comments:

Scoring Key:	R = Resistant to the assistance of others	P = Partial skill (25%–80%)	Use scores alone
	E = Early/emerging skills (1%–25%)	S = Skillful (80%–100%)	or in combination.

Choosing Options and Accommodations for Children • © 1993 by Michael F. Giangreco • Baltimore: Brookes Publishing Co.

VOCATIONAL

PART 1.2

Check only one box:
ASSESS IN PART 1 (Potential Priorities this Year)☐ ASSESS IN PART 2 (Breadth of Curriculum)☒ SKIP FOR NOW☐

		PART 1.3		PART 1.4		PART 2.2
#	ACTIVITIES	SCORE	NEEDS WORK	POTENTIAL PRIORITY	RANK	BREADTH OF CURR.
74	Does Classroom and/or Home Job(s).		N Y			✓
75	Does Job(s) at School, beyond the Classroom, with Peers without Disabilities (e.g., delivers attendance, messages, lunch money; helps operate bookstore or concession).		N Y			
FOR SECONDARY STUDENTS: COMMUNITY WORK SITES						
76	Travels to and from Work Site.		N Y			
77	Uses Time Clock or Check-In Procedure.		N Y			
78	Interacts Appropriately with Coworkers, Customers, and Supervisors.		N Y			
79	Follows Work Site Rules for Safety, Conduct, and Appearance.		N Y			
80	Does Work Independently that is at a Nonfrustrational Level.		N Y			
81	Works with Others (e.g., cooperates, does enough work, accepts assistance, gives assistance).		N Y			
82	Follows Schedule of Work Activities.		N Y			
83	Uses Work Site Leisure Facilities (e.g., engages in appropriate breaktime and lunchtime routines).		N Y			
84	Applies for Job (e.g., finds potential jobs, contacts employers, fills out forms, interviews).		N Y			
			N Y			
			N Y			

Comments:

Scoring Key:	R = Resistant to the assistance of others	P = Partial skill (25%–80%)	Use scores alone
	E = Early/emerging skills (1%–25%)	S = Skillful (80%–100%)	or in combination.

PART 1.5 CROSS-PRIORITIZATION

Transfer a maximum of the top five priorities from each assessed area in their ranked order.

#	Communication	Socialization	Personal Management	Leisure/ Recreation	Applied Academics
1	Describes	Shares	Mobile within + between rooms		Reads symbols
2	Asks Questions	Takes turns	Manages Personal Belongings		Writes name
3	Sustains Communication	Maintains Approp. Behavior	Eats with utensils	Not Assessed	Counts
4	Greets others	Offers Assistance	Responds to Emergency alarm		
5					

(Left margin: R A N K)

#	Home	School	Community	Vocational	Other ( )
1					
2	Not Assessed	Not Assessed	Not Assessed	Not Assessed	
3					
4					
5					

(Left margin: R A N K)

INFORMATION TO SHARE WITH THE FAMILY: First, the family will be asked to rank a maximum of the top eight overall. **Second,** the interviewer verifies the reason for the selection of the priority and assigns a number corresponding to a valued life outcome. **Third,** the family is asked to verify that their selections accurately reflect their priorities. **Fourth,** the participants negotiate which of the ranked priorities should be restated as annual goals and be "Included in the IEP," which should be considered for inclusion as part of the "Breadth of Curriculum," or which should be primarily a "Home" responsibility. **Fifth,** the interviewer will explain how the results of Part 1 will be used and what comes next.

Rank	OVERALL PRIORITIES	Write # Valued Life Outcomes	Included in the IEP	Breadth of Curriculum	Home
1	Shares with Others	2,3	✓		
2	Describes events, objects, Interactions...	4	✓		
3	Mobility within and between rooms	2,4	✓		
4	Manages personal belongings (glasses, hearing aids)	4		✓	
5	Asks questions of others	2,3,4	✓		
6	Reads Symbols (large print letters)	2		✓	
7	Greets others	3		✓	
8	Eats with Utensils	4			

Choosing Options and Accommodations for Children • © 1993 by Michael F. Giangreco • Baltimore: Brookes Publishing Co.

Goal # _1_ (Rank # _1_ from Part 1.5)

Behavior _Shares toys_

Context _In play situation with peers_

Team Member Suggestions _____

Final Goal Statement _In play situation with peers, Keisha will share toys when requested by a peer_

Goal # _2_ (Rank # _2_ from Part 1.5)

Behavior _Describes events, objects, interactions, etc._

Context _In all school situations_

Team Member Suggestions _____

Final Goal Statement _In all school situations (e.g., class, lunch, recess, bus) Keisha will describe recent events, interactions, etc._

Goal # _3_ (Rank # _3_ from Part 1.5)

Behavior _Mobility within and between rooms_

Context _In school_

Team Member Suggestions _In the school building Keisha will find her way on the playground_

Final Goal Statement _In the school setting (building and grounds), Keisha will find her way to places she uses (e.g. cafeteria, class, playground)_

Goal # _4_ (Rank # _5_ from Part 1.5)

Behavior _Asks questions_

Context _In school to peers and adults_

Team Member Suggestions _Focus on peers to get at social interaction_

Final Goal Statement _In school settings and activities, Keisha will ask questions of peers (e.g., "Do you want to play?"; "Can I have a turn"; "What did you do last night?")_

Goal # _____ (Rank # _____ from Part 1.5)

Behavior _____

Context _____

Team Member Suggestions _____

Final Goal Statement _____

PART 2.2   BREADTH OF CURRICULUM WORKSHEET

① Student's name _Keisha Murphy_ _____ Grade being planning for _Kindergarten_

Approximate number of available instructional hours/periods per day = _2½_

Curriculum Areas To Consider	④ How many of the **learning outcomes** in each curriculum area are potentially appropriate for student instruction this school year? (Check appropriate boxes.)				⑤ Target To Teach? ("+" or "–") see criteria	⑥ Source of Curriculum for Target Areas (e.g., general education scope and sequences, COACH activity item numbers)
	MOST (80%–100%)	SOME (20%–80%)	FEW (<20%)	MULTI-LEVEL		
② GENERAL EDUCATION CURRICULUM, GRADE _Kindergarten_ ③ Social/Emotional	✓				+	Central Ave. Kindergarten Curr.
Work Habits	✓				+	Should
Physical Development	✓				+	target at
Art/Music	✓				+	least partial
Language	✓				+	participation
Reading Readiness	✓				+	in all general
Math Development	✓				+	education
Science + Social Studies	✓				+	curriculum
Computer	✓				+	content (see
						attached)
CROSS-ENVIRONMENTAL CURRICULUM Communication[a]			✓		–	
Socialization[a]			✓		–	
Personal Management			✓		–	
Recreation/Leisure	✓				+	COACH #38
Applied Academics[a]		✓			–	
Other						
ENVIRONMENT-SPECIFIC CURRICULUM: Home			✓		–	
School	✓				–	
Community			✓		–	
Vocational[a]			✓		+	COACH #74

[a]Likely overlap with some portion of general education curriculum.

(#) = order in which steps of this worksheet are completed.

Choosing Options and Accommodations for Children • © 1993 by Michael F. Giangreco • Baltimore: Brookes Publishing Co.

148

Student's name _Keisha Murphy_ Planning for the _1991-1992_ school year

Do you agree that the following learning outcomes will be *targeted for instruction*? Write a "+" if you agree. Write a "−" if you disagree. Add other learning outcomes you feel should be targeted for instruction in the blank spaces.

#	Curriculum Area	Learning Outcomes	JM HM	WB	JC	KC	BL	SE	MB	RA
1	Social	Attends to personal needs	+	+	+	+	+	+	+	+
2	Emotional	Cares for materials / belongings	+	+	+	+	+	+	+	+
3		Tries new things	+	+	+	+	+	+	+	+
4		Works and plays independently	+	+	+	+	+	+	+	+
5		Seeks appropriate attention	+	+	+	+	+	+	+	+
6		Respects property, rights of others	+	+	+	+	+	+	+	+
7		Listens courteously	+	+	+	+	+	+	+	+
8		Shows self control	+	+	+	+	+	+	+	+
9		~~Uses pleasant tone of voice~~	−	−	+	−	+	−	−	+
10		Has made friends in school	+	+	+	+	+	+	+	+
11		Exhibits self confidence	+	+	+	+	+	+	+	+
12	↓	Adjusts to new situations	+	+	+	+	+	+	+	+
13	Work Habits	Works to ability	+	+	+	+	+	+	+	+
14		Completes activities	+	+	+	+	+	+	+	+
15		Takes pride in work	+	+	+	+	+	+	+	+
16		Follows directions	+	+	+	+	+	+	+	+
17		Changes easily from one activity to another	+	+	+	+	+	+	+	+
18		Cleans up	+	+	+	+	+	+	+	+
19		Is enthusiastic about learning	+	+	+	+	+	+	+	+
20		Has good attention span	+	+	+	+	+	+	+	+
21	↓	Initiates activities	+	+	+	+	+	+	+	+

Student's name ___Keisha Murphy___ Planning for the ___1991–1992___ school year

Do you agree that the following learning outcomes will be *targeted for instruction*? Write a "+" if you agree. Write a "−" if you disagree. Add other learning outcomes you feel should be targeted for instruction in the blank spaces.

#	Curriculum Area	Learning Outcomes	JM/HM	WB	JL	KC	BL	SE	MB	RA
22	Art	Explores art media	+	+	+	+	+	+	+	+
23	Music	Shows enthusiasm for music	+	+	+	+	+	+	+	+
24	Computer	Types name on keyboard	+	+	+	+	+	+	+	+
25	"	Locates letters/numbers on keyboard	+	+	+	+	+	+	+	+
26	Language	Expresses Ideas	+	+	+	+	+	+	+	+
27		Uses adequate vocabulary	+	+	+	+	+	+	+	+
28		Tells story in sequence	+	+	+	+	+	+	+	+
29	↓	Listens and comprehends	+	+	+	+	+	+	+	+
30	Reading Readiness	Shows interest in books	+	+	+	+	+	+	+	+
31		Participates in choral reading, songs, fingerplay	+	+	+	+	+	+	+	+
32		Names colors	+	+	+	+	+	+	+	+
33		Recognizes own name	+	+	+	+	+	+	+	+
34		Prints name and alphabet	+	+	+	+	+	+	+	+
35		Recognizes alphabet	+	+	+	+	+	+	+	+
36		Associates letters with sounds	+	+	+	+	+	+	+	+
37	↓	Recognizes similarities in words	+	+	+	+	+	+	+	+
38	Math	Counts and recognizes numerals	+	+	+	+	+	+	+	+
39		Names shapes	+	+	+	+	+	+	+	+
40	↓	Sorts and makes patterns	+	+	+	+	+	+	+	+
41	Science + Social Studies	Makes observations	+	+	+	+	+	+	+	+
42	"	Asks questions and draws conclusions	+	+	+	+	+	+	+	+

PART 2.2 BREADTH OF CURRICULUM
LISTING (continued)

Student's name _Keisha Murphy_ Planning for the _1991-1992_ school year

Do you agree that the following learning outcomes will be *targeted for instruction*? Write a "+" if you agree. Write a "−" if you disagree. Add other learning outcomes you feel should be targeted for instruction in the blank spaces.

#	Curriculum Area	Learning Outcomes	JM/HM	WB	JL	KC	BL	SE	MB	RA
43	Science + Social Studies	Engages in active leisure w/peers	+	+	+	+	+	+	+	+
44	Vocational	Does classroom job	+	+	+	+	+	−	+	+

PART 2.3 GENERAL SUPPORTS

Student's name _Keisha Murphy_ Planning for the _1991-1992_ school year
What general supports need to be provided for the student to allow him or her access to learning
opportunities or pursuit of learning outcomes? Write a "+" if you agree. Write a "−" if you disagree.
Write the numbers of corresponding valued life outcome(s) 1–5. Add other general supports you feel
are necessary in the blank spaces.

Category	#	Supports/Accommodations	Valued Life Outcome	Initials of Team Members							
				JM/HM	WB	JL	KC	BL	SE	MB	BA
Personal Needs											
Physical Needs											
Sensory Needs	1	Position close to activity	2+4	+	+	+	+	+	+	+	+
	2	Enlarge materials	2+4	+	+	+	+	+	+	+	+
	3	Use auditory trainer	2+3	+	+	+	+	+	+	+	+
Teaching Others About the Student	4	Teach students and staff about Keisha's communication + behavior	3	+	+	+	+	+	+	+	+
Providing Access and Opportunities												

FAMILY-CENTERED PRIORITIES FOR IEP GOALS (FROM PART 1.5)

COMMUNICATION	1. Describes events, objects, interactions and so forth.
	2. Asks questions of others.
SOCIALIZATION	3. Shares with others.
PERSONAL MANAGEMENT	4. Has mobility within and between rooms.

BREADTH OF CURRICULUM LEARNING OUTCOMES (FROM PART 2.2)

(Based on Kindergarten Curriculum used in the Chittenden East School District, Richmond, Vermont.)

SOCIAL/EMOTIONAL	5. Attends to personal needs.
	6. Cares for materials (including glasses and hearing aids).
	7. Tries new things.
	8. Works and plays independently.
	9. Seeks appropriate attention.
	10. Respects property, rights, feelings of others.
	11. Listens courteously.
	12. Shows self-control.
	13. Makes friends in school.
	14. Shows self-confidence.
	15. Adjusts to new situations.
WORK HABITS	16. Works to ability.
	17. Completes activities.
	18. Takes pride in work.
	19. Follows directions.
	20. Changes easily from one activity to another.
	21. Cleans up.
	22. Is enthusiastic about learning.
	23. Increases attention span.
	24. Initiates activities.
ART	25. Explores art media.
MUSIC	26. Shows enthusiasm for music.
COMPUTER	27. Types name on keyboard.
	28. Locates letters and numbers on the computer keyboard.
LANGUAGE	29. Expresses ideas.
	30. Expands vocabulary.
	31. Tells story in sequence.
	32. Listens and comprehends.

(continued)

READING READINESS

33. Shows interest in books.
34. Participates in choral readings, songs, finger play, and so forth.
35. Names colors.
36. Recognizes own name.
37. Prints name and letters of the alphabet.
38. Associates letters with sounds.
39. Recognizes similarities in words.

MATH

40. Counts and recognizes numerals.
41. Identifies/names shapes.
42. Sorts and makes patterns.

SCIENCE AND SOCIAL STUDIES
RECREATION/LEISURE

43. Makes observations.
44. Asks questions and draws conclusions.
45. Engages in active leisure with peers.

GENERAL SUPPORTS (FROM PART 2.3)

SENSORY NEEDS

46. Position close to activities/people so she can see them.
47. Enlarge materials.
48. Use auditory trainer.

TEACHING OTHERS

49. Teach staff and peers about her communication and behavior.

PART 3.4 SCHEDULING MATRIX

General Class Activities

Student's name: Keisha Murphy
Grade: Kindergarten

		Arrival	Opening Circle	Learning Centers	Journals	P.E./Library	Art/Music	Snack	Recess	Group Projects	Depart
		15 min.	15 min.	30 min.	15 min.	20 min.	20 min.	15 min.	20 min.	20 min.	10 min.
IEP Goals	Describing	1									→
	Asks questions		2								→
	Shares with others	3	3						3	3	
	Mobility within + between rooms	4									→
Breadth of Curriculum	Social/Emotional										
	Work Habits										
	Art										
	Music										
	Computer										
	Language										
	Reading Readiness										
	Math										
	Science/Social Studies										
	Recreation/Leisure	45				45					
General Supports	Sensory Needs	47-49								45	→
	Teaching Others	Addressed situationally									

Note written across curriculum rows: All general education learning outcomes are to be addressed as they are and at the same times as for the students without disabilities, with adaptations as needed. Learning outcomes are to be included in class activities as for all students

Use activity numbers corresponding to Program-at-a-Glance.

Choosing Options and Accommodations for Children • © 1993 by Michael F. Giangreco • Baltimore: Brookes Publishing Co.

PART 3.4   SCHEDULE
for Keisha Murphy

(P = IEP Priority; BC = Breadth of Curriculum; GS = General Supports)

EDUCATIONAL COMPONENTS TO BE ADDRESSED IN EVERY ACTIVITY
(These will not be repeated under each activity.)

(P)   Describes events, objects, interactions, and so forth.
(P)   Asks questions of others.
(P)   Provides mobility within and between rooms.
(GS) Position close to activities/people so she can see them.
(GS) Enlarge materials.
(GS) Use auditory trainer as needed.
(GS) Teach staff and peers about her communication and behavior (to be addressed situationally).

EDUCATIONAL COMPONENTS TO BE ADDRESSED IN SELECTED ACTIVITIES

GENERAL EDUCATION CLASS/ACTIVITY	STUDENT LEARNING OUTCOMES AND SUPPORTS	
ARRIVAL	(P)	Shares with others.
	(BC)	Engages in active leisure/play with others.
LEARNING CENTERS	(P)	Shares with others.
PHYSICAL EDUCATION	(BC)	Engages in active/leisure play with others.
RECESS	(P)	Shares with others.
	(BC)	Engages in active leisure/play with others.
GROUP PROJECTS	(P)	Shares with others.

All other Breadth of Curriculum learning outcomes are to be addressed in the same ways and at the same times as for students without diabilities, with adaptations as needed. Learning outcomes are to be integrated into class activities for all students.

Appendix E

Secondary Student with a Cognitive Impairment (Complete Example)

APPENDIX E: STUDENT DESCRIPTION

Max Mosley is 17 years old and attends 11th grade at River Valley High School. He lives with his parents. He has two older siblings who no longer live at home. Max enjoys visiting his relatives with his parents. He functions in the moderate range of cognitive impairment and has been described as having autistic tendencies (e.g., self-stimulatory behaviors, some echolalic speech). He can respond to questions and use verbal language, but sometimes says things out of context, such as repeating a television commercial when a cafeteria worker asks him which vegetable he wants with his lunch. He can do most basic living skills (e.g., dressing, personal care), but often needs reminders about when to do them and regarding the quality with which they are done. Max enjoys playing basketball and playing catch with a football or baseball. He likes watching movies and game shows on television and tinkering with small motors and other mechanical devices. A few friends from school visit him at his home occasionally, but he spends quite a bit of time alone in his room or in the yard. Max is anxious in crowds and can become physically aggressive in these situations, especially if they are very loud. This has limited his attending a variety of school and community events (e.g., dances, student parties, ball games).

CHOOSING OPTIONS AND ACCOMMODATIONS FOR CHILDREN

COACH

Student's name ___Max Mosley___ Date of birth ___4-30-74___

Date of Family Prioritization Interview (COACH, Part 1) ___5-19-91___

Person interviewing the family ___Karen Sampras___

Educational placement(s) ___Going into Grade 11___

PURPOSE AND DIRECTIONS: In the spaces provided write the names of all team members and their relationship to the student. The "Date reviewed" column is used to indicate the date the results of COACH are shared and reviewed with each team member. It is neither desirable nor necessary for all team members to participate in the completion of COACH (Part 1). Therefore the "Date of Family Prioritization Interview (COACH, Part 1)" will be different from the "Date reviewed" for team members who were not present. This review provides a method for documenting the exchange of important educational information among all team members.

Name of team member	Relationship to student	Date reviewed
Sarah Mosely	Mother	5/19/91
Richard Mosely	Father	5/20/91
Karen Sampras	Special Educ. Teacher	5/19/91
Louise Staples	School Psychologist	5/19/91
Ken Masterson	Speech-Language Pathologist	5/20/91
Gail Kaster	Homeroom Teacher	5/20/91
Carey Ost	Instructional Assistant	5/21/91

Choosing Options and Accommodations for Children • © 1993 by Michael F. Giangreco • Baltimore: Brookes Publishing Co.

PART 1
FAMILY PRIORITIZATION INTERVIEW
INTRODUCTION

The following headings represent categories of information and sample statements to be shared with participants. YOU ARE ENCOURAGED TO INDIVIDUALIZE THE INFORMATION TO FIT EACH FAMILY YOU INTERVIEW. Figures 1, 2, and 3 can be used to illustrate some points.

PURPOSE OF THE FAMILY PRIORITIZATION INTERVIEW

"The purpose of this meeting is to identify the top learning priorities for [student's name] that you [parent] believe would improve [his/her] life. We will also determine which of the selected priorities you feel should be included on the IEP."

"We have asked you [parent] to participate in this meeting because we recognize that you have an important role to play in determining educational priorities for [student's name]."

CONTENT

"The areas we will explore in today's meeting are meant to extend or augment general education curricula. COACH includes a variety of curriculum areas that are designed to improve [student's name] valued life outcomes." See Figure 1.

EXPLAIN WHAT IS GOING TO HAPPEN

TIME

"Today's meeting will take approximately 1 hour" (to complete Parts 1.1–1.5).

RATE

"During that hour, I will be asking you a variety of questions. Since there are so many areas to consider, I want you to be aware that I will be presenting questions rather quickly and will ask for relatively short answers from you."

PARENT OPPORTUNITIES TO DISCUSS PRIORITIES IN DEPTH

"Since some of the questions I ask you will be more important than others, I will ask you to go through each area rather quickly so that we can focus on what you think is important. Once we know what you think is important, then we can plan to spend more time discussing those areas in greater detail after we complete Part 1 or at another time."

OUTCOMES

"By the end of today's meeting you will have selected what you believe are the top priorities for [student's name] to improve [his/her] valued life outcomes. We will discuss and decide which of these priorities should be included on the IEP."

RELATIONSHIP OF PRIORITIES TO THE REST OF THE SCHOOL PROGRAM

"While focusing on [student's name] top educational priorities is important, these priorities represent only one part of the educational program. We realize that [student's name] also needs to have a broad school experience. This will be addressed in Part 2 where we will consider other learning outcomes to be taught (Breadth of Curriculum) and general supports needed to improve [student's name] valued life outcomes." See Figures 2 and 3.

NEXT STEPS

"After today's meeting, we will review your priorities with other team members who were not here today. Once each member is aware of the priorities, we will develop goals, objectives, and the classroom schedule of activities."

PART 1.1 VALUED LIFE OUTCOMES

> **INFORMATION TO SHARE WITH THE FAMILY:** An underlying assumption of COACH is that students' lives should be better as result of being in school. **The purpose of Part 1.1 is to provide a context so the subsequent parts of COACH can be directly related to valued life outcomes.** The following list shows five valued life outcomes that have been identified by families whose children have disabilities:
>
> 1. Having a Safe, Stable Home in Which To Live
> 2. Having Access to a Variety of Places and Engaging in Meaningful Activities
> 3. Having a Social Network of Personally Meaningful Relationships
> 4. Having a Level of Personal Choice and Control that Matches One's Age
> 5. Being Safe and Healthy
>
> The following questions obtain information about the student's current and desired future status related to the valued life outcomes. These questions set a context for subsequent parts of COACH, and are not to generate in-depth discussion. After this information is collected, the family is asked to indicate which valued life outcomes they wish to have emphasized in the school program during the coming year. Therefore, spend only 10–15 minutes having the family briefly answer the questions. **Reword the questions** to match the individual situation. A summary of the family's responses is recorded in the spaces provided.

#1: HAVING A SAFE, STABLE HOME IN WHICH TO LIVE

1. Where does [student's name] live currently (e.g., at home with family, foster home, community residence)?

   Home with parents

   (NOTE: Since this information may already be known, you can record the answer and restate it to the family: "OK, we know that [student's name] lives with you and his sister"; then move on to question 2.)

2. If everything goes as you hope, do you anticipate that [student's name] will continue to live where [she/he] is throughout the school years?

   yes

   If not, what would be a desirable place?

3. Would you like to talk about what a desirable place would be for [student's name] to live as an adult, or is that too far in the future to discuss at this time?

   yes

   If yes, where?   *Supervised apartment*

4. Is there any place you would like to avoid having [student's name] live in the future?

   Institution or large group home

(continued)

PART 1.1   VALUED LIFE OUTCOMES
(continued)

#2: HAVING ACCESS TO A VARIETY OF PLACES AND ENGAGING IN MEANINGFUL ACTIVITIES

5. Where does [student's name] go, and what kinds of activities does [he/she] do that [he/she] likes or make [him/her] feel good about [himself/herself]? Does [student's name] go where the family goes, following the family routine? *He loves sports events + games but doesn't go anymore due to behavior outbursts; difficulty in crowds; likes to play ball, listen to music; he is interested in and fixates on any type of fan or blower; loves animals.*

6. Would you like to see these places and/or activities change or expand in the near future? If so, how? *Wish we could take him everywhere without having to worry about outbursts, especially hockey and basketball games. More types of leisure activities.*

7. ASK THIS QUESTION ONLY IF THE STUDENT IS 13 YEARS OLD OR OLDER. Have you given any thought to what kinds of activities [student's name] might do or places [he/she] might go as a young adult? For example, in the future how might [student's name] spend [his/her] time that is now spent in school (e.g., competitive work, supported work, volunteering, continuing education?) *Supported work*

#3: HAVING A SOCIAL NETWORK OF PERSONALLY MEANINGFUL RELATIONSHIPS

8. Besides [his/her] family, whom does [student's name] have friendships or personal relationships with (e.g., relatives, classmates, friends)? *Cousins, staff at school, a few school friends.*

9. Would you like to see these relationships change or expand in the near future, and if so, how? *Wish he had friends who wanted to do things with him out of school.*

(continued)

PART 1.1 VALUED LIFE OUTCOMES
(continued)

#4: HAVING A LEVEL OF PERSONAL CHOICE AND CONTROL THAT MATCHES ONE'S AGE

10. What, if anything, would you like to see change in [student's name] current level of personal choice and control that would enable [him/her] to pursue a more enjoyable life? *Wonder if some of his aggression is related to this question. He does his own thing calmly unless directed by others to do things.*

#5: BEING SAFE AND HEALTHY

11. What, if anything, would you like to see change in [student's name] current health or safety that would enable [him/her] to pursue a more enjoyable life? *Toileting issues—problems with cleanliness. Doctors want to try him on "behavior" medication — we'd like to avoid that.*

WHICH OUTCOMES SHOULD BE EMPHASIZED?

Now, ask the family, "Which of the outcomes do you feel should be emphasized during this school year? Although all of the outcomes may be important, please pick a maximum of three." **Put a check in the appropriate space in the right-hand column.**

#1: Having a Safe, Stable Home in Which To Live	Emphasize this Year? _____

#2: Having Access to a Variety of Places and Engaging in Meaningful Activities	Emphasize this Year? __✓__

#3: Having a Social Network of Personally Meaningful Relationships	Emphasize this Year? __✓__

#4: Having a Level of Personal Choice and Control that Matches One's Age	Emphasize this Year? __✓__

#5: Being Safe and Healthy	Emphasize this Year? _____

COMMUNICATION[a]

PART 1.2

Check only one box:
ASSESS IN PART 1 (Potential Priorities this Year)☒ ASSESS IN PART 2 (Breadth of Curriculum)☐ SKIP FOR NOW☐

#	ACTIVITIES	PART 1.3 SCORE	NEEDS WORK	PART 1.4 POTENTIAL PRIORITY	RANK	PART 2.2 BREADTH OF CURR.
1	Indicates Continuation or Expresses More (e.g., makes sound or movement when desired interaction stops to indicate he or she would like eating, playing, and so forth to continue).	S	Ⓝ Y			
2	Makes Choices when Presented with Options.	S	Ⓝ Y			
3	Makes Requests (e.g., for objects, food, inter- actions, activities, assistance).	P	N Ⓨ	✓	3	✓
4	Summons Others (e.g., has an acceptable way to call others to him or her).	S	Ⓝ Y			
5	Expresses Rejection/Refusal (e.g., indi- cates when he or she wants something to stop or does not want something to begin).	P	N Ⓨ	✓	4	✓
6	Greets Others.	S	Ⓝ Y			
7	Follows Instructions (e.g., simple, one-step, or multi-step directions).	P	N Ⓨ	✓	1	IEP
8	Describes Events, Objects, Interactions, and so forth (e.g., uses vocabulary, nouns, verbs, adjectives).	P	N Ⓨ	✓	5	✓
9	Responds to Questions (e.g., if asked a question he or she will attempt to answer).	S	Ⓝ Y			
10	Asks Questions of Others.	P	N Ⓨ			✓
11	Sustains Communication with Others (e.g., takes turns, maintains attention, stays on topic, perseveres).	P	N Ⓨ	✓	2	✓
			N Y			
			N Y			

Comments: ③ Asks for the same 2 or 3 things all the time.
⑤ Sometimes gets upset.

Scoring   R = Resistant to the assistance of others   P = Partial skill (25%–80%)   Use scores alone
Key: E = Early/emerging skills (1%–25%)   S = Skillful (80%–100%)   or in combination.

[a]Communication may be exhibited or received in any combination of ways (e.g., speaking, gestures, signing, keyboards).

Choosing Options and Accommodations for Children • © 1993 by Michael F. Giangreco • Baltimore: Brookes Publishing Co.

SOCIALIZATION

PART 1.2

Check only one box:
ASSESS IN PART 1 (Potential Priorities this Year) ☒ ASSESS IN PART 2 (Breadth of Curriculum) ☐ SKIP FOR NOW ☐

#	ACTIVITIES	SCORE	NEEDS WORK	POTENTIAL PRIORITY	RANK	BREADTH OF CURR.
				PART 1.3	**PART 1.4**	**PART 2.2**
12	Reacts to Objects, Activities, and/or People by Displaying Observable Change in Behavior.	S	Ⓝ Y			
13	Initiates Social Interactions.	P	N Ⓨ			
14	Sustains Social Interactions.	E	N Ⓨ	✓	4	✓
15	Terminates Social Interactions.	E	N Ⓨ	✓	5	✓
16	Distinguishes and Interacts Differently with Familiar People, Acquaintances, and Strangers.	P	N Ⓨ	✓		✓
17	Maintains Socially Acceptable Behavior when Alone and/or with Others.	E–P	N Ⓨ	✓	3	✓
18	Accepts Assistance from Others.	S	Ⓝ Y			
19	Offers Assistance to Others.	P	Ⓝ Y			
20	Accepts Transitions Between Routine Activities.	S	Ⓝ Y			
21	Accepts Unexpected Changes in Routine.	P	N Ⓨ	✓	2	
22	Shares with Others.	P–S	Ⓝ Y			
23	Takes Turns.	P–S	Ⓝ Y			
added	Copes with crowded places or activities	E–R	N Ⓨ	✓	1	
			N Y			
			N Y			

Comments:

Scoring   R = Resistant to the assistance of others   P = Partial skill (25%–80%)   Use scores alone
Key: E = Early/emerging skills (1%–25%)   S = Skillful (80%–100%)   or in combination.

Choosing Options and Accommodations for Children • © 1993 by Michael F. Giangreco • Baltimore: Brookes Publishing Co.

PERSONAL MANAGEMENT

PART 1.2

Check only one box:
ASSESS IN PART 1 (Potential Priorities this Year) ☒ ASSESS IN PART 2 (Breadth of Curriculum) ☐ SKIP FOR NOW ☐

#	ACTIVITIES	PART 1.3 SCORE	NEEDS WORK	PART 1.4 POTENTIAL PRIORITY	RANK	PART 2.2 BREADTH OF CURR.
24	Drinks and Eats by Mouth (e.g., accepts food/drink, lip closure, chews, swallows).	S	Ⓝ Y			
25	Feeds Self with Hands/Fingers.	S	Ⓝ Y			
26	Eats with Utensils (e.g., spoon, fork, knife)	S	Ⓝ Y			
27	Dresses/Undresses.	P	N Ⓨ			
28	Cares for Bowel and Bladder Needs.	P-R	N Ⓨ	✓	1	
29	Cares for Hands and Face (e.g., washes, dries, applies lotion, lip balm, blows nose).	S	Ⓝ Y			
30	Combs/Brushes Hair.	S	Ⓝ Y			
31	Gives Self-Identification Information (e.g., name, address, telephone number)	P-S	Ⓝ Y			
32	Responds to Emergency Alarm (e.g., leaves building when smoke/fire alarm sounds).	P	N Ⓨ	✓	2	
33	Manages Personal Belongings (e.g., toys, clothes, special equipment).	P	N Ⓨ	✓	3	IEP
34	Mobile Within and Between Rooms of a Building (e.g., walks, rolls, crawls, moves wheelchair, climbs stairs, uses elevators/escalators).	S	Ⓝ Y			
			N Y			
			N Y			
			N Y			
			N Y			

Comments:

Scoring Key: R = Resistant to the assistance of others   P = Partial skill (25%–80%)   Use scores alone
E = Early/emerging skills (1%–25%)   S = Skillful (80%–100%)   or in combination.

Choosing Options and Accommodations for Children • © 1993 by Michael F. Giangreco • Baltimore: Brookes Publishing Co.

LEISURE/RECREATION

PART 1.2

Check only one box:
ASSESS IN PART 1 (Potential Priorities this Year) ☒ ASSESS IN PART 2 (Breadth of Curriculum) ☐ SKIP FOR NOW ☐

#	ACTIVITIES	PART 1.3 SCORE	NEEDS WORK	PART 1.4 POTENTIAL PRIORITY	RANK	PART 2.2 BREADTH OF CURR.
35	Engages in Individual, Passive Leisure Activities (e.g., listens to music, watches television).	S	Ⓝ Y			
36	Engages in Individual, Active Leisure Activities (e.g., toy play, games, sports, exercise, hobbies).	P	Ⓝ Y			
37	Engages in Passive Leisure Activities with Others (e.g., goes to movies, performances, spectator sports or events with others).	E-R	N Ⓨ	✓	1	
38	Engages in Active Leisure with Others (e.g., group games, activities, sports).	E-P	N Ⓨ	✓	2	
			N Y			
			N Y			
			N Y			
			N Y			

Comments:

Scoring Key: R = Resistant to the assistance of others   P = Partial skill (25%–80%)   Use scores alone
E = Early/emerging skills (1%–25%)   S = Skillful (80%–100%)   or in combination.

APPLIED ACADEMICS[a]

COACH

PART 1.2

Check only one box:
ASSESS IN PART 1 (Potential Priorities this Year) ☒ ASSESS IN PART 2 (Breadth of Curriculum) ☐ SKIP FOR NOW ☐

		PART 1.3		PART 1.4		PART 2.2
#	ACTIVITIES	SCORE	NEEDS WORK	POTENTIAL PRIORITY	RANK	BREADTH OF CURR.
39	Reads Individual Symbols or Sequences of Symbols (e.g., letters, words, Braille, Bliss, Picsyms).	P	N ⓨ	✓	2	✓
40	Reads To Get Information and/or Follow Instructions.	P	N ⓨ	✓	3	✓
41	Writes Self-Identification Information (e.g., name, address, telephone number).	P	N ⓨ	✓	4	IEP
42	Writes Words, Phrases, Sentences.	P	N ⓨ	✓	5	✓
43	Composes and Writes Notes, Messages, and/or Correspondence.	E	Ⓝ Y			
44	Uses Resource Materials (e.g., newspaper, address book, telephone book, dictionary).	E	Ⓝ Y			
45	Counts with Correspondence.	S	Ⓝ Y			
46	Computes Numbers (e.g., add, subtract, multiply, divide).	P-S	Ⓝ Y			
47	Uses Clock (e.g., face clock, digital, alarm).	P-S	Ⓝ Y			
48	Uses Calendar (e.g., can determine day/date, uses to note special events/ appointments).	P-S	Ⓝ Y			
49	Uses Measurement Tools (e.g., ruler, measuring cups, scale).	P-S	Ⓝ Y			
50	Uses Money (e.g., purchasing, saving, budgeting, checking).	P	N ⓨ	✓	1	IEP
51	Uses Telephone (e.g., answers, calls, uses public pay telephone).	P	N ⓨ			
			N Y			
			N Y			

Comments:

Scoring   R = Resistant to the assistance of others   P = Partial skill (25%–80%)   Use scores alone
Key: E = Early/emerging skills (1%–25%)   S = Skillful (80%–100%)   or in combination.

[a] *"Reading and Writing"* may extend beyond written words to other forms (e.g., braille, keyboarding, computers)

Choosing Options and Accommodations for Children • © 1993 by Michael F. Giangreco • Baltimore: Brookes Publishing Co.

HOME

PART 1.2

Check only one box:
ASSESS IN PART 1 (Potential Priorities this Year) ☐ ASSESS IN PART 2 (Breadth of Curriculum) ☒ SKIP FOR NOW ☐

		PART 1.3		PART 1.4		PART 2.2
#	ACTIVITIES	SCORE	NEEDS WORK	POTENTIAL PRIORITY	RANK	BREADTH OF CURR.
52	Brushes/Flosses Teeth.		N Y			
53	Selects Appropriate Clothing To Wear (e.g., selects items needed for time of day, weather conditions, style matching).		N Y			
54	Cares for Personal Hygiene Needs (e.g., bathes, showers, cares for nails, uses deodorant, shaves).		N Y			
55	Picks Up After Self.		N Y			
56	Prepares Food (e.g., snacks, cold meals, hot meals).		N Y			
57	Does Household Chores (e.g., dusts, sweeps, mops, vacuums, washes/dries dishes, takes out garbage, recycles, makes bed, stores groceries, yardwork).		N Y			
58	Cares for Clothing (e.g., puts laundry in designated place when clean or dirty, folds, washes/dries, irons, mends).		N Y			
			N Y			
			N Y			
			N Y			
			N Y			

Comments:

Scoring	R = Resistant to the assistance of others	P = Partial skill (25%–80%)	Use scores alone
Key:	E = Early/emerging skills (1%–25%)	S = Skillful (80%–100%)	or in combination.

Choosing Options and Accommodations for Children • © 1993 by Michael F. Giangreco • Baltimore: Brookes Publishing Co.

SCHOOL

PART 1.2

Check only one box:
ASSESS IN PART 1 (Potential Priorities this Year)☐ ASSESS IN PART 2 (Breadth of Curriculum)☒ SKIP FOR NOW☐

			PART 1.3		PART 1.4		PART 2.2
#	ACTIVITIES	SCORE	NEEDS WORK	POTENTIAL PRIORITY	RANK	BREADTH OF CURR.
59	Travels to and from School (e.g., rides bus safely, walks to school).		N Y			
60	Participates in Small Groups (e.g., tolerates situation, takes turn, is actively involved, responds to teacher directions).		N Y			
61	Participates in Large Groups (e.g., tolerates situation, takes turn, is actively involved, responds to teacher directions).		N Y			✓
62	Works at Task Independently at Nonfrustrational Level (e.g., starts, sustains, completes).		N Y			✓
63	Manages School-Related Belongings (e.g., backpack, materials, books, hall locker, gym equipment and locker).		N Y			*IEP*
64	Follows School Rules/Routines (e.g., understands what rules are, raises hand, waits turn, no hitting, follows schedule).		N Y			✓
65	Uses School Facilities (e.g., playground, cafeteria, library).		N Y			✓
66	Participates in Extra-Curricular Activities (e.g., clubs, sports, service organizations, drama, music).		N Y			✓
			N Y			
			N Y			
			N Y			
			N Y			
			N Y			

Comments:

Scoring	R = Resistant to the assistance of others	P = Partial skill (25%–80%)	Use scores alone
Key:	E = Early/emerging skills (1%–25%)	S = Skillful (80%–100%)	or in combination.

Choosing Options and Accommodations for Children • © 1993 by Michael F. Giangreco • Baltimore: Brookes Publishing Co.

COMMUNITY

PART 1.2

Check only one box:
ASSESS IN PART 1 (Potential Priorities this Year) ☐ ASSESS IN PART 2 (Breadth of Curriculum) ☒ SKIP FOR NOW ☐

		PART 1.3		PART 1.4		PART 2.2
#	ACTIVITIES	SCORE	NEEDS WORK	POTENTIAL PRIORITY	RANK	BREADTH OF CURR.
67	Travels Safely in the Community (e.g., crosses intersections, uses crosswalks and sidewalks, acts appropriately with strangers, finds destination).		N Y			✓
68	Visits Restaurants (e.g., orders food, finds seating, eats meal, pays bill).		N Y			
69	Purchases Merchandise or Services (e.g., food stores, clothing/department stores, specialty stores, post office, hair salon, laundry/dry cleaner; knows purpose of different kinds of stores, finds merchandise or service desired, pays bill).		N Y			*IEP*
70	Uses Recreational Facilities (e.g., movies, arcades, parks, recreation centers).		N Y			
71	Uses Vending Machines (e.g., to get drinks, food, toys, stamps, newspapers).		N Y			
72	Uses Banking Facilities (e.g., deposits, withdrawals, uses automated teller machines).		N Y			
73	Travels by Public Transportation (e.g., bus, subway, trolley, taxi, ferry).		N Y			✓
			N Y			
			N Y			
			N Y			

Comments:

Scoring   R = Resistant to the assistance of others   P = Partial skill (25%–80%)   Use scores alone
Key: E = Early/emerging skills (1%–25%)   S = Skillful (80%–100%)   or in combination.

Choosing Options and Accommodations for Children • © 1993 by Michael F. Giangreco • Baltimore: Brookes Publishing Co.

VOCATIONAL

PART 1.2

Check only one box:
ASSESS IN PART 1 (Potential Priorities this Year) ☒   ASSESS IN PART 2 (Breadth of Curriculum) ☐   SKIP FOR NOW ☐

#	ACTIVITIES	PART 1.3 SCORE	NEEDS WORK	PART 1.4 POTENTIAL PRIORITY	RANK	PART 2.2 BREADTH OF CURR.
74	Does Classroom and/or Home Job(s).	P	Ⓝ Y			
75	Does Job(s) at School, beyond the Classroom, with Peers without Disabilities (e.g., delivers attendance, messages, lunch money; helps operate bookstore or concession).	P	N Ⓨ			
FOR SECONDARY STUDENTS: COMMUNITY WORK SITES						
76	Travels to and from Work Site.	E	N Ⓨ	✓	4	✓
77	Uses Time Clock or Check-In Procedure.	S	Ⓝ Y			
78	Interacts Appropriately with Coworkers, Customers, and Supervisors.	E-P	N Ⓨ	✓	2	IEP
79	Follows Work Site Rules for Safety, Conduct, and Appearance.	E-P	N Ⓨ			✓
80	Does Work Independently that is at a Nonfrustrational Level.	P	N Ⓨ	✓	3	✓
81	Works with Others (e.g., cooperates, does enough work, accepts assistance, gives assistance).	P	N Ⓨ			✓
82	Follows Schedule of Work Activities.	E	N Ⓨ	✓	1	✓
83	Uses Work Site Leisure Facilities (e.g., engages in appropriate breaktime and lunchtime routines).	P	N Ⓨ			✓
84	Applies for Job (e.g., finds potential jobs, contacts employers, fills out forms, interviews).	E	Ⓝ Y			
			N Y			
			N Y			

Comments:

Transfer a maximum of the top five priorities from each assessed area in their ranked order.

#	Communication	Socialization	Personal Management	Leisure/ Recreation	Applied Academics
1	Follows Instructions	Copes with Crowds	Cares for Bowel Needs	Passive Leisure w/others	Uses Money
2	Sustains Communication	Accepts Un-expected changes	Responds to Emergency Alarm	Active leisure w/others	Reads words
3	Makes choices	Maintains behavior	Manages personal belongings		Reads to get information
4	Expresses refusal	Sustains Interactions			Writes self ID information
5	Describes Events, etc.	Terminates Interactions			Writes words, phrases

RANK

#	Home	School	Community	Vocational	Other ( )
1				Follows work schedule	
2				Interacts with co-workers	
3		NOT			
4		ASSESSED			
5					

RANK

INFORMATION TO SHARE WITH THE FAMILY: First, the family will be asked to rank a maximum of the top eight overall. **Second,** the interviewer verifies the reason for the selection of the priority and assigns a number corresponding to a valued life outcome. **Third,** the family is asked to verify that their selections accurately reflect their priorities. **Fourth,** the participants negotiate which of the ranked priorities should be restated as annual goals and be "Included in the IEP," which should be considered for inclusion as part of the "Breadth of Curriculum," or which should be primarily a "Home" responsibility. **Fifth,** the interviewer will explain how the results of Part 1 will be used and what comes next.

		Write #	Check only one box for each priority		
Rank	OVERALL PRIORITIES	Valued Life Outcomes	Included in the IEP	Breadth of Curriculum	Home
1	Copes with Crowds (Passive leisure)	2			✓
2	Maintains appropriate behavior	2+3		✓	
3	Interacts appropriately with co-workers	2+3	✓		
4	Follows instructions	5	✓		
5	Manages personal belongings	4	✓		
6	Uses money	2+4	✓		
7	Writes self-identification information	4+5	✓		
8	Sustains interactions	3		✓	

Choosing Options and Accommodations for Children • © 1993 by Michael F. Giangreco • Baltimore: Brookes Publishing Co.

PART 2.1 ANNUAL GOAL WORKSHEET
(Use as needed.)

Goal # ___1___ (Rank # ___3___ from Part 1.5)

Behavior _Interact with co-workers by greeting, asking, answering questions_

Context _At work site_

Team Member Suggestions _____

_____

Final Goal Statement _At a community work site Max will interact with co-workers by greeting and asking/answering age-appropriate questions_

Goal # ___2___ (Rank # ___4___ from Part 1.5)

Behavior _Follows instructions_

Context _Related to participation in activities with peers_

Team Member Suggestions _Related to personal safety?_

_____

Final Goal Statement _When in groups with peers involving participating activities, Max will follow instructions that will enhance his participation_

Goal # ___3___ (Rank # ___5___ from Part 1.5)

Behavior _Manages personal belongings_

Context _At school_

Team Member Suggestions _(books, supplies, lunch money, jacket)_

_____

Final Goal Statement _At school Max will manage his personal belongings (e.g., backpack, jacket, books, lunch money) so he has it when needed_

Goal # ___4___ (Rank # ___6___ from Part 1.5)

Behavior _Use money_

Context _Community settings_

Team Member Suggestions _Also in cafeteria and school bookstore_

_____

Final Goal Statement _In purchasing situations (e.g. cafeteria, bus, stores) Max will make small purchases (under $10)_

Goal # ___5___ (Rank # ___7___ from Part 1.5)

Behavior _Writes self-identification information_

Context _In class and community_

Team Member Suggestions _Name, address, phone number_

_____

Final Goal Statement _In class and appropriate community settings Max will sign his name and write his address and phone number._

Choosing Options and Accommodations for Children • © 1993 by Michael F. Giangreco • Baltimore: Brookes Publishing Co.

COACH

① Student's name __Max Mosley__ Grade being planning for __11__

Approximate number of available instructional hours/periods per day = __8 periods__

Curriculum Areas To Consider	④ How many of the **learning outcomes** in each curriculum area are potentially appropriate for student instruction this school year? (Check appropriate boxes.)				⑤ Target To Teach? ("+" or "–") see criteria	⑥ Source of Curriculum for Target Areas (e.g., general education scope and sequences, COACH activity item numbers)
	MOST (80%–100%)	SOME (20%–80%)	FEW (<20%)	MULTI-LEVEL		
② GENERAL EDUCATION CURRICULUM, GRADE __11__ ③ Algebra / Trig			✓		–	River Valley Curriculum
Chemistry			✓		–	
English 11			✓		–	
American History			✓		–	
Health				✓	+	12, 27, 28, 37
Physical Educ.		✓			+	1, 4, 24, 27
Computer Science			✓			
Elective (Photography)				✓	+	10, 11, 16, 21
Vocational Educ.	✓				–	
CROSS-ENVIRONMENTAL CURRICULUM Communication[a]		✓			+	COACH #s 3, 5, 8, 10, 11
Socialization[a]		✓			+	COACH #s 14-17
Personal Management			✓		–	
Recreation/Leisure			✓		–	
Applied Academics[a]		✓			+	COACH #s 39, 40, 42
Other						
ENVIRONMENT-SPECIFIC CURRICULUM Home			✓		–	
School		✓			+	COACH 61, 62, 64-66
Community			✓		+	COACH 67, 73
Vocational[a]		✓			+	COACH 76, 79-83

[a]Likely overlap with some portion of general education curriculum.

(#) = order in which steps of this worksheet are completed.

Choosing Options and Accommodations for Children • © 1993 by Michael F. Giangreco • Baltimore: Brookes Publishing Co.

Student's name ___Max Mosley___   Planning for the ___1991-1992___ school year
Do you agree that the following learning outcomes will be *targeted for instruction*? Write a "+" if you agree. Write a "−" if you disagree. Add other learning outcomes you feel should be targeted for instruction in the blank spaces.

#	Curriculum Area	Learning Outcomes	SM	RM	KS	LS	KM	GK	CO	
1	Health	Understands effects of smoking	+	+	+	+	+	+	+	
2	"	Understands how disease is spread	+	+	+	+	+	+	+	
3	"	Knows 2 ways to reduce spread of disease	+	+	+	+	+	+	+	
4	"	Knows effects of alcohol and drugs	+	+	+	+	+	+	+	
5	Phys. Educ.	Participates in group activities	+	+	+	+	+	+	+	
6	"	Follows game rules	+	+	+	+	+	+	+	
7	"	Displays "sporting" behavior	+	+	+	+	+	+	+	
8	"	Increases cardiovascular endurance	+	+	+	+	+	+	+	
9	Photography	Loads film in camera	+	+	+	+	+	+	+	
10	"	Takes photos of people	+	+	+	+	+	+	+	
11	"	Takes photos of scenes/events	+	+	+	+	+	+	+	
12	"	Maintains photo album	+	+	+	+	+	+	+	
13	Communication	Makes requests	+	+	+	+	+	+	+	
14	"	Summons others	−	+	−	+	−	−	+	
15	"	Describes events, etc.	+	+	+	+	+	+	+	
16	"	Asks questions of others	+	+	+	+	+	+	+	
17	"	Sustains Communication	+	+	+	+	+	+	+	
18	Socialization	Initiates Interactions	−	+	−	−	−	−	+	
19	"	Sustains Interactions	+	+	+	+	+	+	+	
20	"	Terminates Interactions	+	+	+	+	+	+	+	
21	"	Maintains Appropriate behavior	+	+	+	+	+	+	+	

Choosing Options and Accommodations for Children • © 1993 by Michael F. Giangreco • Baltimore: Brookes Publishing Co.

Student's name __Max Mosley__ Planning for the __1991–1992__ school year

Do you agree that the following learning outcomes will be *targeted for instruction*? Write a "+" if you agree. Write a "–" if you disagree. Add other learning outcomes you feel should be targeted for instruction in the blank spaces.

#	Curriculum Area	Learning Outcomes	SM	RM	KS	LS	KM	GK	CO	
22	Academics	Reads Symbols	+	+	+	+	+	+	+	
23	"	Reads to get information	+	+	+	+	+	+	+	
24	"	Writes words + phrases	+	+	+	+	+	+	+	
25	School	Participates in large groups	+	+	+	+	+	+	+	
26	"	Works at task independently	+	+	+	+	+	+	+	
27	"	Follows school rules/routines	+	+	+	+	+	+	+	
28	"	Uses school facilities	+	+	+	+	+	+	+	
29	"	Participates in Extra-curr. Activities	+	+	+	+	+	+	+	
30	Community	Travels safely in community	+	+	+	+	+	+	+	
31	"	Travels by public transportation	+	+	+	+	+	+	+	
32	Vocational	Travels to and from work site	+	+	+	+	+	+	+	
33	"	Follows work site rules	+	+	+	+	+	+	+	
34	"	Does work independently	–	–	+	–	–	–	+	
35	"	Works with others	+	+	+	+	+	+	+	
36	"	Follows schedule of work act.	+	+	+	+	+	+	+	
37	"	Uses work site leisure facilities	+	+	+	+	+	+	+	

Choosing Options and Accommodations for Children • © 1993 by Michael F. Giangreco • Baltimore: Brookes Publishing Co.

COACH

Student's name _____Max Mosley_____ Planning for the _1991-1992_ school year

What general supports need to be provided for the student to allow him or her access to learning opportunities or pursuit of learning outcomes? Write a "+" if you agree. Write a "−" if you disagree. Write the numbers of corresponding valued life outcome(s) 1–5. Add other general supports you feel are necessary in the blank spaces.

Category	#	Supports/Accommodations	Valued Life Outcome	Initials of Team Members							
				SM	RM	KS	LS	KM	GK	CO	
Personal Needs		None Needed									
Physical Needs		None Needed									
Sensory Needs		None Needed									
Teaching Others About the Student	1	Staff must know Crisis Intervention Plan if aggressive in large groups	2+3	+	+	+	+	+	+	+	
Providing Access and Opportunities		None Needed									

PART 2.4. COACH-GENERATED PROGRAM-AT-A-GLANCE
for Max Mosley

FAMILY-CENTERED PRIORITIES FOR IEP GOALS (FROM PART 1.5)

COMMUNICATION	1. Follows instructions.
PERSONAL MANAGEMENT	2. Manages personal belongings.
APPLIED ACADEMICS	3. Uses money.
	4. Writes self-identification information.
VOCATIONAL	5. Interacts appropriately with coworkers.

BREADTH OF CURRICULUM LEARNING OUTCOMES (FROM PART 2.2)

HEALTH	6. Understands negative effects of smoking.
	7. Knows how disease is spread.[a]
	8. Knows two ways to reduce the spread of disease.[a]
	9. Understands the negative effects of alcohol and drugs.
PHYSICAL EDUCATION	10. Participates in group activities.
	11. Follows game rules.
	12. Shows "sporting" behavior.
	13. Increases cardiovascular endurance.
PHOTOGRAPHY	14. Loads film in a camera.
	15. Takes photographs of people.
	16. Takes photographs of scenes or events.
	17. Maintains photo album.
COMMUNICATION	18. Makes requests.
	19. Describes, events, objects, interactions.
	20. Asks questions of others.
	21. Sustains communication with others.
SOCIALIZATION	22. Sustains interactions with others.
	23. Terminates interactions with others.
	24. Maintains appropriate behavior.
APPLIED ACADEMICS	25. Reads symbols.
	26. Reads to get information.
	27. Writes words and phrases.
SCHOOL	28. Participates in large groups.
	29. Works at task independently.
	30. Follows school rules and routines.
	31. Uses school facilities.
	32. Participates in extra-curricular activities.
COMMUNITY	33. Travels safely in the community.
	34. Travels by public transportation.[a]
VOCATIONAL	35. Travels to community work site.[a]
	36. Follows work site rules for safety, conduct, and appearance.
	37. Works with others.
	38. Follows schedule of work activities.
	39. Uses work site leisure facilities.

---

[a]To be addressed later in the school year

(continued)

PART 2.4.   COACH-GENERATED PROGRAM-AT-A-GLANCE
for Max Mosley (*continued*)

GENERAL SUPPORTS (FROM PART 2.3)

TEACHING OTHERS

40. Staff must know crisis intervention plan if he becomes aggressive in large group situations.

COACH

PART 3.4   SCHEDULING MATRIX

Student's name _Max Mosley_

Grade _11_

General Class Activities

		Home Room	Algebra	Chem.	Eng.	Amer. Hist.	Health	Lunch	P.E.	Comp.	Photo	Voc.	Year Book / Extra Curr.
		15 min.	45 min.	45 min.	45 min.	45 mn.	45 min.	45 min.	45 min.	45 min.	45 min.	135 min.	60 m.
IEP Goals	Follows Instructions	1	1	1	1	1	1	1	1	1	1	1	1
	Manages personal belongings	2	2	2	2	2	2	2	2	2	2	2	2
	Uses money							3				3	
	Writes self-ID info.		4	4	4	4	4			4	4	4	4
	Interacts with co-workers											5	5
Breadth of Curriculum	Health						6-9						
	Physical Education								10-13				
	Photography										14-17		14-16
	Communication	18-21	→										
	Socialization	22-24	→										
	Applied Academics		25-27			→	→	25-26	→	25-27			
	School	30	29-30			→	→	28-31 / 31		29-31	29-31	29-36	
	Community											33	
	Vocational											36-39	36-39
General Supports	Teaching others about the student	All staff members must be oriented and taught about the team's crisis intervention plan before working with Max											

Use activity numbers corresponding to Program-at-a-Glance.

Choosing Options and Accommodations for Children • © 1993 by Michael F. Giangreco • Baltimore: Brookes Publishing Co.

PART 3.4 SCHEDULE
for Max Mosley

(P = IEP Priority; BC = Breadth of Curriculum; GS = General Supports)

EDUCATIONAL COMPONENTS TO BE ADDRESSED IN EVERY ACTIVITY
(These will not be repeated under each activity.)

(P)   Follows instructions.
(P)   Manages personal belongings.
(P)   Writes self-identification information.
(BC)   Makes requests.
(BC)   Describes, events, objects, interactions.
(BC)   Asks questions of others.
(BC)   Sustains communication with others.
(BC)   Sustains interactions with others.
(BC)   Terminates interactions with others.
(BC)   Maintains appropriate behavior.
(BC)   Follows school rules and routines.
(GS)   Staff must know crisis intervention plan if he becomes aggressive in large groups.

EDUCATIONAL COMPONENTS TO BE ADDRESSED IN SELECTED ACTIVITIES

GENERAL EDUCATION CLASS/ACTIVITY	STUDENT LEARNING OUTCOMES AND SUPPORTS
HOME ROOM	See "Educational Components To Be Addressed in Every Activity."
1st PERIOD CHEMISTRY	See "Educational Components To Be Addressed in Every Activity." (BC) Reads symbols. (BC) Reads to get information. (BC) Writes words and phrases. (BC) Works at task independently.
2nd PERIOD PHYSICAL EDUCATION	See "Educational Components To Be Addressed in Every Activity." (BC) Participates in group activities. (BC) Follows game rules. (BC) Shows "sporting" behavior. (BC) Increases cardiovascular endurance. (BC) Participates in large groups. (BC) Works at task independently. (BC) Uses school facilities.
3rd PERIOD HEALTH	See "Educational Components To Be Addressed in Every Activity." (BC) Understands negative effects of smoking. (BC) Understands the negative effects of alcohol and drugs. (BC) Reads symbols. (BC) Reads to get information. (BC) Writes words and phrases. (BC) Works at task independently.

(*continued*)

PART 3.4. SCHEDULE
for Max Mosley(*continued*)

(P = IEP Priority; BC = Breadth of Curriculum; GS = General Supports)

4th PERIOD PHOTOGRAPHY	See "Educational Components To Be Addressed in Every Activity." (BC) Loads film in camera. (BC) Takes photographs of people. (BC) Takes photographs of scenes/events. (BC) Maintains photograph album. (BC) Reads symbols. (BC) Reads to get information.
5th PERIOD LUNCH	See "Educational Components To Be Addressed in Every Activity." (P) Uses money. (BC) Participates in large groups. (BC) Uses school facilities.
6th–8th PERIOD COMMUNITY VOCATIONAL	See "Educational Components To Be Addressed in Every Activity." (P) Uses money. (P) Interacts appropriately with coworkers. (BC) Travels safely in the community. (BC) Follows work site rules for safety, conduct, and appearance. (BC) Works with others. (BC) Follows schedule of work activities. (BC) Uses work site leisure facilities.
Extra-Curricular Activity YEAR BOOK PHOTOGRAPHER (after school)	See "Educational Components To Be Addressed in Every Activity." (BC) Loads film in camera. (BC) Takes photographs of people. (BC) Takes photographs of scenes/events. (BC) Reads symbols. (BC) Reads to get information. (BC) Works at task independently. (BC) Uses school facilities.

INDEX

Page numbers followed by "f" indicate figures or forms; page numbers followed by "t" indicate tables.